THE RISORGIMENTO AND THE UNIFICATION OF ITALY

The Risorgimento and the Unification of Italy was originally published by George Allen & Unwin in 1971 as volume 11 in the *Historical Problems: Studies and Documents* series edited by Professor G.R. Elton.

THE RISORGIMENTO AND THE UNIFICATION OF ITALY

Derek Beales
Professor of Modern History in the University of Cambridge and Fellow of Sidney Sussex College

Longman
London and New York

Longman Group UK Limited
Longman House, Burnt Mill, Harlow
Essex CM20 2JE, England
and Associated Companies throughout the world

Published in the United States of America
by Longman Inc., New York

First published 1971 by George Allen & Unwin in the Historical Problems series
First published by Longman 1981
Ninth impression 1992

British Library Cataloguing in Publication Data

Beales, Derek
The Risorgimento and the unification of Italy.
1. Italy - History - 1848-1870
I. Title
945'.08 DG552

ISBN 0-582-49217-3

Printed in Malaysia by SUB

CONTENTS

MAPS

PREFACE TO THE LONGMAN EDITION

My main purpose in writing this book was to supply an accessible account of the Risorgimento and the unification of Italy which would embody the approach of Denis Mack Smith. It happened that he had never himself provided such an account, except in the necessarily disconnected form of his commentary on the documents in his *Making of Italy*. My own contribution was to emphasize the difficulty of relating the Risorgimento, the national movement, to the actual unification, which appeared to be a function largely of international politics. I was also responsible for the stress laid on the divergence between the idealism of Italian, and the pragmatism of English, historiography.

Although my comments on the Idealism of Italian historiography have attracted criticism,[1] I see no reason to change them, except to remark that Italian writing in the last decade has been less dominated by the patriotic myth.

Nor am I inclined to modify my view that the Risorgimento and unification must be regarded as in large measure distinct. The doctrine of 'the primacy of internal politics', whatever may be thought about it in the case of Germany, cannot possibly be held to apply to the unification of Italy. Students of the history of Italy, whether Italians or not, naturally concentrate on the domestic affairs of the peninsula. It is always difficult to establish the precise connections between external and internal influences and policies. Diplomatic history has been out of fashion. In a magisterial review of recent literature on the Risorgimento in Sicily, especially Rosario Romeo's book of that title, Agatha Ramm wrote in 1972:

'Neither the massive volumes of documents ... nor the exciting intellectual exercise of constructing diplomatic history from the criss-crossing despatches of the international network, nor yet the brilliant interpretations by those with political objectives — none of these can keep the past generally alive for the present generation. Its interest is in whole societies and their operations and it will only accept history, such as Romeo's which responds to this interest.'[2]

Perhaps this is less true in the early 1980s. But whenever I am led to ask myself whether I have underrated the significance of the 1848 revolutions and the activities of their promoters, I see before me again the spectacle of Hungary in 1956 and Czechoslovakia in 1968, and I come back to the view that there are few countries strong and fortunate enough to be able to retain control of their own destinies, especially during revolutionary periods.

However, if I were writing the book afresh, I should try to take account of a number of important contributions which have been published since 1970.

The figure of Franco Venturi towers over contemporary Italian historical writing. As well as numerous articles, he has now published two more volumes of his great work on the intellectual, cultural and social history of the peninsula in the eighteenth century, *Settecento riformatore*. The general effect of this path-breaking study is to raise the importance of the Italian Enlightenment and of the indigenous contribution to it. But the book deals with the age before the Risorgimento rather than with the Risorgimento itself.[3] Some of Venturi's articles have been made available in English translation by S. J. Woolf under the title *Italy and the Enlightenment* (London, 1972).

Apart from Venturi's work — and especially since Romeo's life of Cavour has not yet reached its subject's years of fame — much of the most interesting new material has appeared in English.

Mr Mack Smith himself brought out a collection of essays in 1971, *Victor Emanuel, Cavour, and the Risorgimento*. The volume contains some of his earlier articles, like those on 'Cavour and Parliament', 'Cavour and the Thousand' and 'The Peasants' Revolt in Sicily, 1860' (the last-named translated from Italian) and his 'Outline of Risorgimento History, 1840–1870' from the *New Cambridge Modern History*. It also includes important new work, especially on the role of Victor Emanuel.

J. M. Roberts' *The Mythology of the Secret Societies* (London, 1972) makes it possible to place Buonarroti and Mazzini more firmly in their context.

The most comprehensive single work to appear in this field since 1970 is S. J. Woolf's *A History of Italy 1700–1860: The*

Social Constraints of Political Change (London, 1979). This volume is a translation and enlargement of a section contributed by the author to a new large-scale *Storia d'Italia*. My own reaction to the latter part of the book is that it seems in fact, by the nature of the story, to place its emphasis on the *political* constraints of *social* change. Though Professor Woolf has been asked to write social history, he finds that this genre will not explain the events of 1859–60. But the volume must be ten times longer than mine, and is indispensable for the serious student of the subject. Its greatest strength lies in its successful incorporation of recent Italian work on social history, especially on the period since 1789, to which two-thirds of the book is devoted.

In *Austria and the Papacy in the Age of Metternich*, vol. I, covering 1809–30 (Washington, D. C., 1979), A. J. Reinerman brings out the divergences between these two apparently intimate allies.

Finally, two contrasting books of outstanding interest appeared in 1979, dealing with the revolutions of 1848 in Lombardy and Venetia. A. Sked, in *The Survival of the Habsburg Empire: Radetzky, the imperial army and the class war, 1848*, describes the situation from the Austrian military standpoint. A fascinating comparison can be made with P. Ginsborg, *Daniele Manin and the Venetian Revolution of 1848–49*. Both authors stress the scale of revolutionary fervour in the early months of 1848, which provoked desertions from the Austrian army on the one hand, and on the other, enthusiastic co-operation from representatives of all classes. Sked emphasizes Radetzky's failure to consolidate his military victory by winning the Italians, and especially the peasantry, for the Habsburg cause. Ginsborg, though he dissociates himself from the more simple-minded disciples of Gramsci, comes near to his position, or at least his terms of reference, in his conclusion: 'the failure of the revolution of 1848–9 cast its long shadow over the life of the new nation state.' (p. 379). This failure he attributes largely to the rigid bourgeois attitudes of Manin.

I suspect that both authors exaggerate the extent to which the peasantry could be expected to support any government at all; the adoption of military conscription seems to have been a secure road to unpopularity for any regime. I doubt whether either Radetzky or Manin had much chance of winning friends among the mass of the people. And I fear it remains true that the international situation was decisive for Radetzky's victory and Manin's defeat. But, if I had been writing *The Risorgimento and the Unification of Italy* now, I should certainly have tried to incorporate a more extended discussion of the issues raised by these two stimulating books.

Sidney Sussex College, Cambridge
Christmas Eve, 1980 Derek Beales

1. G. Monsagrati in *Rassegna storica del Risorgimento*, Vol. LIX (1972), pp. 451–2. I have taken some account also of the criticisms of J. Whittam in *History*, Vol. 57 (1972), pp. 452–3. Mr Mack Smith kindly drew my attention to several errors. I should like to draw attention to a full and interesting review article about English writing on the Risorgimento: C. H. Church, 'Storiografia inglese e Risorgimento dopo la II guerra mondiale,' *Rassegna storica del Risorgimento*, Vol. LXII (1975), pp. 163–99. I owe thanks to Dr J. S. Morrill.
2. A. Ramm, 'The Risorgimento in Sicily,' *English Historical Review*, Vol. LXXXVII (1972), pp. 795–811.
3. The first volume, subtitled 'Da Muratori a Beccaria' appeared in Turin in 1969; the second, 'La chiesa e la repubblica dentro i loro limiti,' in 1976; the third, 'La prima crisi dell'Antico Regime, 1768-1776' in 1979. A fourth is planned.

Since I wrote this preface, W.O. Chadwick's *The Popes and European Revolution* (Oxford, 1981) has appeared. By providing a full and sympathetic account of the Italian Church in the eighteenth and early nineteenth centuries, it sets the whole story in a new perspective.

1

Historiography

On the face of it, the unification of Italy happened very quickly, owed much to good fortune, and was largely an affair of war and diplomacy. At the beginning of the year 1859 Italy was divided politically into seven main parts (see Map 5). Six of these were sovereign states in themselves; the seventh, consisting of Lombardy and Venetia, was included within the Austrian Empire. In the previous three centuries, dynasties had been shuffled and boundaries adjusted, but the map of the peninsula had not altered fundamentally – except briefly during two periods of French domination between 1796 and 1815 (Maps 2 and 3). The country had never been united politically since the sixth century. Yet in less than two years, between April 1859 and November 1860, almost the whole of Italy was brought under one ruler, King Victor Emanuel II of Sardinia.

This remarkable outcome followed a short war from April to July 1859 in which, allied with the Emperor Napoleon III of France, Victor Emanuel defeated Austria. As a result she gave up most of Lombardy. Under cover of the war successful revolutions occurred in the states of Central Italy. Then in 1860 Giuseppe Garibaldi led a guerrilla expedition to Sicily and Naples, which drove out their king. Sardinia annexed all these territories (Maps 6a-d). Lord Palmerston, the British Prime Minister, described the result as 'miraculous as no one in his senses or in his dreams could have anticipated such continuous success'.[1]

The only important areas outstanding were Venetia, still Austrian, and a sizable district around the City of Rome, which was what remained of the Papal State. The new Kingdom of Italy fought Austria as the ally of Prussia in 1866, and so won Venetia. Finally, in 1870, as a by-product of the Franco-Prussian War, Italy gained all but 109 acres of the Papal state.

[1] 10 November 1860, Clarendon to Cowley (P.R.O. F.O. 519/178).

Most Italians and Italian historians, however, see unification differently. To them it was not the sudden and accidental upshot of war and diplomacy. It was a result or a stage of their national revival, known as the Risorgimento, which originated in the eighteenth century and has lasted, according to many writers, into the twentieth. This is how Giorgio Candeloro puts it in the most notable recent history of modern Italy by an Italian: 'In common usage the word Risorgimento refers to the movement which led to the formation of the Italian national unitary state.'[2]

This formulation begs the very question which is my chief concern in this Introduction to try to resolve. Certainly there was an Italian national revival, but it seems to me that the precise relationship between Risorgimento and unification is exceedingly hard to determine.

Merely by posing this problem I separate myself from the main tradition of Italian historical writing. This is of course dangerous and might be thought presumptuous, since the enormous majority of works on this subject belong to that tradition. But an English historian, especially one born in the twentieth century, could scarcely find it possible to enter into the spirit of Italian historiography of the Risorgimento. He cannot, in the first place, fully share the patriotic feelings of Italians. And, more serious, his philosophical presuppositions will be different from those of most Italian historians.

English readers ought to know something, however sketchy, of Italian historiography, not only because its tendencies have a long history and themselves help to explain the Risorgimento, but also because it has inevitably guided English historians of Italy. Even before unification, men who wished to make Italians more conscious of their nationality sought their justification in history. Of these Vincenzo Gioberti (Doc. 9) had fantastic but particularly influential views. Since unification, historians and publicists have glorified all who played a part in it, and tried to fit into the story many who have little claim to belong there. Differences among Italians have been played down, the role of Italian soldiers magnified, and the origins of the development pushed further and further back in time. No doubt some such campaign was necessary to the strengthening of Italian feelings of nationhood.

In addition to this generalized myth there have been created party historiographies. The political disputes of the Kingdom (and, after 1946, of the Republic) were related in fact, and rather differently in people's minds, to the divisions of the years before unification. The chief parties concerned had been these: moderate monarchists on the one hand, led by Count Cavour, Prime Minister of Sardinia from 1852

[2] G. Candeloro, *Storia dell'Italia moderna*, Vol. I (Milan, 1956), p. 14.

to 1861 (except for a few months) and first Prime Minister of the Kingdom of Italy; and on the other hand 'radicals', many of them republican and a few socialist, who had looked up to Garibaldi and to Giuseppe Mazzini, conspirator and prophet of nationalism. In the twentieth century matters have become more complicated. Fascism tried to annex the glory of unification to itself; Roman Catholics, their church reconciled at last with the new Kingdom in 1929, began to exalt those of their adherents who had sympathized with the national movement; and socialists both emphasized the role of their forerunners in the Risorgimento and reinterpreted the whole story in terms of their theories of history. All these approaches, when not taken to extremes, have illuminated the study of unification; and the continuing interest in the subject, which is sustained by its relevance for all Italians, has led to the discovery and publication of much important material. Sometimes, though, grave distortion has resulted, and there have occurred cases of deliberate falsification.[3]

Much Italian historiography, further, differs fundamentally from English in its philosophical standpoint. In Italy history is commonly studied in conjunction with philosophy, and Idealist philosophers are taken much more seriously than in England. The Italian language, too, is peculiarly apt for rhetoric. The greatest exemplar here is Benedetto Croce. His immense output included many works which the most matter-of-fact English historian must admire, such as the untranslated *Storia di Napoli*. But he also perpetrated *History as the Story of Liberty*. G. M. Young was exceptionally receptive, as English historians go, to Idealist attitudes, but he began his review of it as follows: 'I should find it easier to write of Croce's book if I had the least idea what it was all about.' Much of it, he said, was 'only the wallowing of the balloon among the clouds'.[4] An English historian had translated it, but some of it cannot be made to sound like sense in English. Walter Maturi, much less of a philosopher than Croce, described the Risorgimento as 'essentially an ethico-politico-national myth'.[5] Luigi Salvatorelli, equally moderate, wrote:

'From Bettinelli to Carducci, from Alfieri to Gioberti, from the Jacobin patriots to Santarosa, from Mazzini to Cavour, all—whether they used the specific term, or expressed the concept in other words—understood by Risorgimento of Italy a fact, or better a process, of a

[3] For an extreme example see C. Quigley, 'Falsification of a Source in Risorgimento History', *Journal of Modern History*, 1948.

[4] G. M. Young, 'Benedetto Croce' in *Last Essays* (London, 1950), pp. 41–6. Quotations from pp. 41, 45.

[5] From the article in the *Enciclopedia italiana* (1936) on Risorgimento.

spiritual character, an intimate and thorough transformation of national life, an affirmation of collective and individual autonomy. Of course, the name had first an exclusively or primarily literary and cultural significance and later assumed also a political and territorial significance. Italy and Risorgimento have both been understood, over the centuries, as before all else facts of consciousness, as spiritual attitudes.'[6]

This, to an English historian, is merely a more grandiose way than Candeloro's of begging the main question.

Philosophical Idealism asserts that ideas (meaning here 'abstract concepts', such as that of Italian nationhood) are the true 'concrete reality' and the proper object of historical study, because in the end they are destined to 'embody themselves' in institutions, such as the Italian State. Historians who accept this view necessarily disbelieve that chances or accidents may have important consequences. They are inclined to suppose that conscious thought commonly achieves its aims and that right in some sense always triumphs. This high-flown metaphysic clashes violently with English pragmatism. I can illustrate the point best by referring to an Italian review of a work of my own. In writing of British policy towards Italy at the time of unification I remarked that the play of chance and the interaction of half-blind forces contributed much to the outcome. The reviewer accused me of adopting the heresies not only of Denis Mack Smith, the principal living English historian of Italy, but also those of both Sir Lewis Namier and Sir Herbert Butterfield. Scholars who in the English context are thought to be at opposite poles seem from the Italian viewpoint to be scarcely distinguishable and equally wrong.[7]

Marxism has profoundly affected Italian historiography of the Risorgimento in the last twenty years, in large measure through the writings of Antonio Gramsci, most of which were composed while he was a prisoner of the Fascists. He believed that the moderates had contrived at the time of unification to deny to the radicals a fair share of the fruits of an achievement to which both parties had contributed. He particularly stressed the role of the peasantry in nineteenth-century Italian history and described the Risorgimento in what has become a famous phrase as 'an agrarian revolution *manquée*'. But he combated one idealism with another.

'The Risorgimento [he wrote] is a complex and contradictory historical development, which issues as a unity from all its antithetical

[6] L. Salvatorelli, *Pensiero e Azione del Risorgimento* (Turin, 1943), p. 5.

[7] G. Giarrizzo, review of D. Beales, *England and Italy, 1859–60* (London, 1961) in *Rivista storica italiana* 1961, pp. 819–26.

elements, from its protagonists and its antagonists, from their struggles, from the reciprocal modifications which the struggles themselves impose, and also from the action of the passive and latent forces like the great agrarian masses, and further, naturally, from the pre-eminent role of international relations.'[8]

The unification of Italy, then, is a subject which poses for the student the most fundamental historiographical questions, and he has to bear in mind that English attitudes to them are different from Italian. Shifts of outlook within the tradition of English historical writing on Italian unification are less momentous. But they deserve notice. The literature is not voluminous, but it stands comparison with English work on any other European country, and with the work on Italy of historians from other non-Italian countries. Many of the largest and most notable volumes date from the last years of the nineteenth century and the early years of the twentieth. Bolton King's *History of Italian Unity* was published in 1899, and, best-known of all the books in the canon, G. M. Trevelyan's trilogy on Garibaldi appeared between 1907 and 1911. These writings testify to the interest of English Liberals in the new State, and show a tendency, similar to that in Italian historiography of the same period, to see the whole history of Italy in the nineteenth century in relation to unification. The emphasis was somewhat different, of course. Less was said of military glory, and there was less philosophical verbiage. More was said about the achievements of representative government in Italy. In 1911 Trevelyan wrote this peroration to *Garibaldi and the Making of Italy*:

Nothing is more remarkable—though to believers in nationality and ordered liberty nothing is more natural—than the stability of the Italian Kingdom. . . . The building is as safe as any in Europe. . . . The power of this great national movement has fortunately been directed only to the securing of Italian liberty, and not to the oppression of others. . . . The result has been the unstained purity and idealism of patriotic emotion there. . . . Italy has now been 'neutralized' as securely as Switzerland.[9]

With the war, and the rise of Mussolini to power, there was naturally

[8] A. Gramsci, *Il Risorgimento* (Turin, 1949), p. 108, quoted in A. W. Salomone, 'The *Risorgimento* between Ideology and History: The Political Myth of *rivoluzione mancata*', *American Historical Review* 1962, p. 47n.

[9] G. M. Trevelyan, *Garibaldi's Defence of the Roman Republic* (London, 1907); *Garibaldi and the Thousand* (London, 1909); and *Garibaldi and the Making of Italy* (London, 1911). Quotation from p. 294.

a reaction. Trevelyan himself, in a lecture delivered in 1923, was uneasy in justifying the manner of Mussolini's triumph.

'People sometimes ask me, why could not the Italians have effected the change of government that they desired by means of a general election? It is certainly a very pertinent question. I reply by pointing the inquirer to their social and political history, which had unfitted them for expressing themselves by means of a general election. It is, in my view, very unfortunate that the Italians fail to express the national will at the polling booth, but it is not at all unnatural. . . . In England a general election is a moral earthquake. . . . But in Italy a general election is the sum of a number of obscure intrigues!'[10]

W. K. Hancock was working in Italy at the same period on the book which appeared in 1926 as *Ricasoli and the Risorgimento in Tuscany*. In his autobiography he records that he became critical of Italian nationalism in history because of the revulsion he felt at the manifestations of fascism which he witnessed.[11] These doubts, however, do not appear in A. J. Whyte's *Political Life and Letters of Cavour, 1848–1861* of 1930. On the other hand G. F-H. Berkeley believed that his *Italy in the Making* of 1932–40 could be more detached than earlier histories now that the Papacy had made its peace with the Italian State.[12]

Since the Second World War the decay of Liberal sympathy with nationalism has been illustrated in the work on Italian history of Denis Mack Smith. His *Cavour and Garibaldi 1860*, published in 1954 and using the newly-printed volumes of Cavour's correspondence, emphasized the disputes and uncertainties of Italian patriots during the critical phase of unification. His general history of Italy since 1861, which appeared in 1959, and his history of Sicily since the early Middle Ages, of 1968, have irritated many Italians by their criticism of the church and of the whole established order.[13] In particular, he lacks respect for patriotic grandiloquence and the Italian armed forces. Here is an extract from a review by a senior Italian historian of *Italy: A Modern History*:

[10] *The Historical Causes of the Present State of Affairs in Italy* (Barnett House Papers, No. 8), p. 8, partly quoted in O. Chadwick, *Freedom and the Historian* (Cambridge, 1969), p. 32.

[11] W. K. Hancock, *Country and Calling* (London, 1954), pp. 92–3.

[12] G. F-H. Berkeley, *Italy in the Making, 1815 to 1846* (Cambridge, 1932); (with J. Berkeley,) *Italy in the Making, June 1846 to January 1848* (Cambridge, 1936); (with J. Berkeley,) *Italy in the Making, January 1st 1848 to November 16th 1848* (Cambridge, 1940). See the first volume, p. ix.

[13] D. Mack Smith, *Italy: A Modern History* (London, 1959); *Medieval Sicily: 800–1713* (London, 1968) and *Modern Sicily after 1713* (London, 1968).

'It is not only that there is a prefabricated plan which represents a people perennially merry-making. There is something worse. . . . He reduces the Risorgimento to a peaceful development through fortunate circumstances, to selfish interests, to a complex of material needs, to strokes of fortune and diplomatic deceit, to "student escapades"; that is, he takes away its soul.

The Risorgimento was spirit of sacrifice, it was suffering in the ways of exile and in the galleys, it was blood of Italian youth on the battlefields . . . it was the passion of a people for its Italian identity.'[14]

Other English historians who have recently written substantial works on the Risorgimento, E. E. Y. Hales and Christopher Seton-Watson, have been less critical of the movement.[15] But it is Mack Smith whose researches and outlook have given a new twist to Risorgimento historiography, in Italy as well as in England.[16]

His influence will be apparent throughout this Introduction, the object of which is to give a brief account of Italian history from the origins of the Risorgimento to the achievement of unification, with special reference to the question 'What was the relationship between the national movement and the creation of the Kingdom of Italy?'

[14] N. Rodolico in *Archivio storico italiano* 1960, p. 299.

[15] E. E. Y. Hales, *Pio Nono* (London, 1954) and *Mazzini and the Secret Societies* (London, 1956); C. Seton-Watson, *Italy from Liberalism to Fascism: 1870–1925* (London, 1967).

[16] The best book on Risorgimento historiography is W. Maturi, *Interpretazioni del Risorgimento* (Turin, 1962). S. J. Woolf, *The Italian Risorgimento* (London, 1969), contains a brief historiographical discussion, with extracts. And see, as for this whole Introduction, the progress report on Risorgimento studies published by Marzorati of Milan (editor unnamed): *Nuove Questioni di Storia del Risorgimento e dell'Unità d'Italia* (2 vols, Milan, 1961).

For other works of Denis Mack Smith see the collection of his essays in *Studi Risorgimentali* (ed. V. Frosini), entitled *Da Cavour a Mussolini* (Catania, 1968). His chapter in *The New Cambridge Modern History*, Vol. X (1830–1870) (ed. J. P. T. Bury, Cambridge, 1960), 'Italy', is his nearest approach to a consecutive account of unification. In *The Making of Italy, 1796–1870* (London, 1968) he tells the story through documents, as he has done much more fully in *Il Risorgimento italiano* (Bari, 1968). His *Garibaldi* (London, 1957) is the best English biography, and he has also published a documentary collection on Garibaldi in the Great Lives Observed series (London, 1969).

I have arbitrarily omitted American writing from this account of English historiography of the Risorgimento. The story is not dissimilar, but there is an element present which is absent in England, the work of Americans of Italian origin, such as H. R. Marraro, G. Megaro, E. P. Noether, G. T. Romani, A. W. Salomone and M. Salvadori.

2

The Beginnings of the Risorgimento, to 1815

It is natural to begin the political story in 1748. In that year the Treaty of Aix-la-Chapelle brought to an end the War of the Austrian Succession and inaugurated nearly fifty years of peace in Italy. During this period of stability may be traced the beginnings of the Risorgimento.

From 1748 until the first French invasion in 1796 the number of sizable independent states in Italy was eleven (Map 1). This computation excludes enclaves, tiny principalities and the Republic of San Marino. Easily the largest state was formed by the two kingdoms of Naples and of Sicily, held jointly. They were ruled by a member of the Spanish royal family, a branch of the Bourbons, but separately from Spain. Hence Charles III of Naples, when he succeeded to the throne of Spain in 1759, gave up his Italian kingdoms. One other kingdom was largely Italian, that of Sardinia. This state comprised the island of Sardinia and a compact territory on the mainland straddling the modern Franco-Italian border. It included the original home of the dynasty, the Duchy of Savoy, which was French-speaking and since 1860 has mostly belonged to France. But by the mid-eighteenth century the heart of the kingdom was the area in Italy known as Piedmont. The island of Sardinia had been added only in 1718–20. By the Treaty of Aix-la-Chapelle the state acquired a slice of the Duchy of Milan. In the rest of this Introduction the Kingdom of Sardinia will be called, as is usual, simply 'Piedmont'.

There still survived three ancient republics of importance: Venice, ruling a considerable empire on the eastern shores of the Adriatic and a large territory, known as the Veneto, on the mainland of Italy; Genoa, which until 1768 governed the island of Corsica; and Lucca. The Papal State included much of central Italy. Then there were five significant duchies. Of these the two most important were ruled by members of the Austrian royal House of Habsburg, Milan direct from Vienna, and

AUSTRIAN EMPIRE
SWISS CONFEDERATION
AVOY
KINGDOM
LOMBARDY
DUCHY OF MILAN
Milan
Turin
PIEDMONT
DUCHY OF PARMA
REPUBLIC OF GENOA
Genoa
DUCHY OF MODENA
Romagna (Legations)
Venice
R.Po
REPUBLIC OF VENICE
OTTOMAN EMPIRE
ADRIATIC SEA
DUCHY OF MASSA & CARRARA
REP. OF LUCCA
Pisa
Florence
GRAND DUCHY OF TUSCANY
Leghorn
Siena
PAPAL STATES
APENNINES
GULF OF
CORSICA (To Genoa)
SARDINIA
ISLAND OF SARDINIA
Rome
KINGDOM OF NAPLES (with Sicily)
Naples
MEDITERRANEAN SEA
Palermo
KINGDOM OF SICILY (with Naples)
Tunis
MALTA

taly in 1748

Tuscany separately. The Duchy of Parma and Piacenza was under a Spanish Bourbon, but could not be united either with Spain or with Naples and Sicily. The Duke of Modena and the Duchess of Massa and Carrara represented Italian dynasties.

Politically, then, Italy was fragmented. Further, half the states were governed by kings or dukes who already occupied or hoped soon to inherit the thrones of non-Italian countries. Venice and Piedmont had dominions outside Italy. The Papacy had worldwide ecclesiastical concerns. The peninsula was not merely divided; the boundaries and interests of its states ignored its natural frontiers.

The obvious parallel is with Germany at the same period, which was much more fragmented, into over three hundred states. But in some respects the Italian situation seemed even less favourable to national aspirations than the German. The Holy Roman Empire gave some semblance of political unity to an area corresponding roughly with Germany, whereas Italy had no political meaning at all. Further, Italy displayed a unique range of constitutions. The Papal State presented a special problem. And more than half the peninsula had received new dynasties since 1700: Naples and Sicily, the island of Sardinia, Milan, Tuscany, Parma and Piacenza. Italy was the laboratory of dynasticism.

According to Prince Metternich, Austrian Chancellor in the early nineteenth century, Italy was, if nothing more, at least a 'geographical expression'. But, though her natural frontiers are exceptionally well-defined, geography divides her internally. The chief physical feature is the Apennine range, which makes communication across the peninsula difficult throughout its length. Most of the rivers are of little use for navigation, being torrents in the winter and trickles in the summer. There is a broad contrast between the only large area of plain in the country, the Po valley, and the mountainous remainder. The coastline is enormously long, and in most places a narrow fertile belt near the sea gives way quickly to barren hill inland.

These divisions, it will be noticed, do not match the state boundaries of the eighteenth century. Genoa is manifestly distinct from Corsica, and Piedmont from the island of Sardinia. Less obviously, within the Papal State the area east of the Apennines, and particularly the northern part near the delta of the Po, which was known interchangeably as 'the Romagna' or 'the Legations', was the natural associate of the Veneto rather than of Rome and its environs. It was no doubt partly for geographical reasons that Romagnuol opposition to the rule of the popes was to be important in nineteenth-century Italian history.

Furthermore, differences of outlook corresponded with neither political nor geographical divisions. Sicilians felt the bitterest antagonism against Neapolitans, and clearly the reasons were mainly historical. Sicily had been politically separate from Naples and Italy for much of its history. It preserved the only parliament in Italy to survive into the eighteenth century. The government at Naples tended to treat Sicily as a colony, economically as well as politically. The Sicilians reacted by obstructing the policies of their rulers. Quite often they broke into open revolt. The particularism of Sicily was even more important in nineteenth-century Italian history than that of the Romagna. In the North, the inhabitants of the Veneto believed themselves to be exploited by the government of the Republic based in Venice. But it was not these comparatively large-scale clashes which were necessarily the most significant. The English traveller in Italy, accustomed to something approaching uniformity of style in the architecture of his own country at any given period of its history, is astonished by the contrasts between the buildings, say, of thirteenth-century Pisa, Siena and Florence, which are only fifty miles apart. This observation points to the fact that in Italy, not only then but also later, the patriotism of many was focused on their city or even on their village. This is what Italians call *campanilismo*, which means 'parochialism' in its original sense, the cult of the parish (Doc. 6).

Even this is not the end of the tale of division. Within some states there were enclaves belonging to others. Within all there were numerous customs barriers, hindering trade for the sake of fiscal advantage. In 1750 there were 498 such impediments in Piedmont alone.[1] Italy was a geographical expression of limited significance only.

Anything that can properly be called Italian nationalism was lacking in the mid-eighteenth century. In the sixteenth century there had been some evidence of it. Machiavelli had denounced the Papacy as the principal obstacle to Italian political unity, and urged some secular prince to work to that end. Since his time the cry had scarcely been heard. Educated persons remained conscious of the literary tradition of the Italian language and were aware of being Italians, but the church worshipped and administered, and the universities taught, in Latin. It was probably a factor delaying the growth of Italian national feeling that Italians annexed to their own history that of classical Rome. There was no society or newspaper catering for the whole of Italy. When academies were founded, as they were in great numbers in the eighteenth century, they were locally based. When the arts prospered, it was in a particular state, usually because of the patronage of the court: opera in Naples under Charles III; architecture in Piedmont in the early years of the century, and in Rome later; the *commedia dell'arte* and

[1] *Nuove Questioni*, Vol. I, p. 252.

painting in Venice. In one part of Italy, Piedmont, Italian was barely known; either French or the local dialect were used (Doc. 1). For the uneducated Italy and the Italian language meant nothing. They spoke dialects incomprehensible to people from other parts of the peninsula.[2]

Throughout this book it will be necessary to keep in mind the distinctions between nationalism, liberalism and reformism. The term 'nationalism' itself covers a variety of phenomena. A nation is essentially a social and cultural unit, that is, it is defined by the attitudes of men rather than by the provisions of laws and treaties. Unless a body of individuals think of themselves as a nation, there is no nation. They need not have a state, a country, a religion, even a language to themselves. They may not belong to one race. Equally, a state may rule several nations, or only part of one. A nation may be divided religiously, a religion nationally. Those who speak a particular language may belong to two or more nations. Races are so impure that it is hardly possible to distinguish them. The only common bond essential to a nation, by definition, is culture. For 'nationalism' to exist, however, there must be a measure of self-assertion about the nation. There must at a minimum be an emphasis on the unity and distinctness of the national culture. Nationalism varies in intensity. There is likely to develop a feeling that the nation ought to have only one language, and that all those who speak that language as their mother-tongue should regard themselves as belonging to the nation. There may appear a desire for religious uniformity within the nation. It may be demanded that the nation be identified with a state. In the extreme case nationalists insist that their countrymen and the state associated with their nation should dominate over others. At least there is bound to be a tension between the ideal of the nation-state and the realities of nationality. The pure nation-state, embracing all members of the nation in a territorial unity, excluding all aliens, requiring uniformity of religion, language and culture, cannot exist.

'Liberalism' is also an imprecise term. It must include some element of a claim for liberty. The main kinds of liberty involved are political and religious: free speech, freedom of worship, perhaps the more positive freedom embodied in political representation. Free trade may also be a Liberal demand. Liberalism is in theory, though not always in practice, distinct from nationalism. Though some thinkers like Mazzini have seen national freedom, that is, some form of political status for the

[2] The most useful references in English are E. P. Noether, *Seeds of Italian Nationalism* (New York, 1951); B. Migliorini, *The Italian Language* (London, 1966); and R. Wittkower, *Art and Architecture in Italy, 1600–1750* (London, 1965).

nation, as the essential precondition of political, religious and economic liberty, others like Acton have believed the two forces to be fundamentally in opposition.

'Reformism' is a less well-established term. I use it in order to make one further distinction. It is possible to seek changes in laws and constitutions in the interests of efficiency or humanity, but without reference to liberty, let alone to nationality. It will sometimes be convenient to call this attitude reformism.

Nationalism cannot be found in the Italy of the middle eighteenth century. But reformism, and a dash of liberalism, can. In the historiography of the period these attitudes are grouped under the heading of 'Enlightenment'. It is necessary to know something of their development and application in Italy in order to understand the Risorgimento. Indeed, any attempt by Italians to improve conditions in their country, even at a local level, may be considered a part of their national revival.

It is difficult to know which was the more remarkable in the eighteenth century, the fragmentation of Italy or her backwardness. In the Middle Ages much of the peninsula had been comparatively rich and populous, and its economy uniquely advanced. There had existed a large number of flourishing towns, with a vigorous communal life. The laity had played a much greater part in political and cultural development than in other European countries. Around 1750 Italy was still relatively populous and urbanized, but she was by no means exceptionally rich. Not only had other countries progressed more rapidly, but the Italian economy had become absolutely depressed. Communal life had decayed, and the laity was probably less influential than in most other parts of Europe, even Roman Catholic Europe.

Italian economic development had at times followed the same course as English or French. Broadly, the late fourteenth century was a period of decline, the late sixteenth century one of advance. But general factors had operated against Italy. The exploitation of ocean trade by those countries with an Altantic coastline had been followed by the irruption of their ships into the Mediterranean. Italian industries had been undercut by those of England and Holland. Wars fought in Italy in the early sixteenth century and the early eighteenth century had done economic damage. The fact that from about 1530 to at least 1700 obscurantist, colonialist Spain dominated the peninsula has been thought by many Italians to have worsened the economic position of their country. Certainly, the development in Europe of the strictly-defined territorial state made it impossible for Italy to continue to prosper as the whole West's banker and trader. In the fifteenth and sixteenth centuries city-states became obsolete, and those that wished to survive had to turn themselves into principalities. Venice and the Papacy both illustrate this tendency, as does Florence under the Medici, eventually absorbing formerly independent cities like Siena. It may be that the peninsula as a whole suffered because several small powers were strong enough to maintain themselves there, assisted by the rivalry between the French Bourbons and the Habsburgs of Spain and Austria, in which Italy was a battlefield. Whatever the reasons, by the middle of the seventeenth century, the decline of Italy was not only relative, but absolute. Population fell. There was a drift from town to country. Industry dwindled. Invisible exports, and earnings from banking and other services—except for ecclesiastical payments—almost disappeared. Commentators agreed that a high proportion of the still large urban population were beggars, and a high proportion of the rural population brigands. The only significant manufacture of eighteenth-century Italy was silk-weaving, in the north. Her only notable exports were raw materials: olive oil, wine, grain, wool and raw silk.[3]

In the twentieth century the most striking regional division in Italy is that between the wealthy, industrialized, materialist, progressive north and the poor, backward, superstitious, conservative south. The origins of this contrast are a matter of impassioned controversy. The distinction appears at the present day to be founded on geographical differences. The modern south not only lacks rain, but also trees and fertile soil. Nonetheless, Naples and Sicily had a widespread reputation for the prodigality of their natural endowment until as late as the nineteenth century (Doc. 4). This, however, would appear to have owed more to classical learning than contemporary information. The south had not participated fully in the industrial, commercial and communal progress of Italy, except perhaps in the early Middle Ages. Naples, the largest city in the peninsula in the eighteenth century, was never an economic centre of the same kind as Genoa or Venice had once been, where money was invested in trade and industry rather than in landed property. Like many other European capitals of the time, it was a place where a court composed of large landowners gathered to spend their money 'unproductively', attracting around them not businessmen but skilled craftsmen, servants and beggars. It did not even boast a town hall. The church owned an exceptionally high proportion of the land in the south. Ecclesiastical and secular lords had much independent

[3] There is a large literature in Italian, and a good deal in French. The most useful English book is B. Pullan (ed.), *Crisis and Change in the Venetian Economy* (London, 1968), which contains a translation of a revised and improved version of the article by C. M. Cipolla, 'The Economic Decline of Italy' which appeared first in *Economic History Review*, 1952.

jurisdiction. What amounted to serfdom was general. Agriculture was less commercialized than in the north. It was sometimes so wasteful that parts of Sicily and Naples had already been reduced from fertility to desert. Geography had to be assisted by human failings to make the south so backward. But the process was well under way by the eighteenth century.[4]

All the same, at no time since the High Middle Ages had the north been so like the south as in the eighteenth century. Agriculture was everywhere dominant. Landownership had displaced commercial enterprise as the pride of the republics. The church and the nobility were entrenched.

During the eighteenth century, revival began. There were signs of it even before 1748. The glory of seventeenth-century Italy had been that she was the headquarters of the Counter-Reformation. Hence her superb Baroque art, and hence her persecution of Galileo. In the 1680s, encouraged by a Spanish viceroy, what was called a 'new civilization' flowered in Naples.[5] When Charles III became King of Naples and Sicily in 1735 he set about improving his state, trying to reduce the power of church and nobility, to codify and reform the law, to reduce taxation and to encourage learning. But even in his case the more effective work was done after 1748, and over Italy as a whole the late eighteenth century was much more 'enlightened' than the early.

The Enlightenment had many aspects. In Italy in the second half of the eighteenth century, where its representatives were numerous and distinguished, its emphases were these. It was strongly rationalist, that is, it trusted in man's reason rather than in revelation or in tradition. Through rational enquiry, it believed, solutions could be found to social, economic and political problems, and the lives of the mass of individuals could be made happier. The church, at least insofar as she was opposed to rational enquiry and supported tradition and superstition for their own sake, or blocked the way to practical reform, was the enemy of the Enlightenment. Many of its followers went further and attacked her theology and her wealth, either because they considered them rationally indefensible or because they objected to them on religious grounds.

[4] In English see R. S. Eckaus, 'The North-South Differential in Italian Economic Development', *Journal of Economic History* 1961; Mack Smith, *Modern Sicily after 1713*. F. Compagna, *La Questione Meridionale* (Milan, 1963) is a useful short summary of the problem.

[5] B. Croce, *Storia del regno di Napoli* (Bari, 1925), p. 145; E. Ghelli, 'Il Vicerè Marchese del Carpio', *Archivio storico per le Province Napoletane* 1933 & 1934. Cf. F. Venturi, 'La Circolazione delle Idee' in *Atti del XXXII Congresso di Storia del Risorgimento italiano* (Rome, 1954), p. 33.

There was a strong element of Jansenism, unorthodox Roman Catholicism, in the movement, and not a little genuine Protestantism.[6]

In Italy the chief centres of the Enlightenment were Florence, Milan and Naples. Its best-known representative was Cesare Beccaria of Milan, whose treatise *Dei delitti e delle pene* ('Of Crimes and Punishments'), published in 1764, became one of the textbooks of the campaign to abolish the death penalty and mitigate the severity of the criminal law all over Europe. Others who deserve special notice are Antonio Genovesi, for whom Charles III created at Naples the first Chair of Political Economy in Europe in 1754, and who was the first teacher in his university to lecture in Italian; and the brothers Pietro and Alessandro Verri, of Milan.

France, however, was acknowledged to be the leading country of the Enlightenment, and for the most part Italy's contribution was derivative. Moreover, the movement there was to some extent artificial. Its character varied from state to state according to the outlook of the rulers; and, where the regime was of long standing or of Italian origin, there was seldom much sign of enlightenment. The Republic of Genoa became a lesser centre of the movement in the second half of the eighteenth century, but with little result so far as the running of the state was concerned. Venice and, more understandably, the Papacy were affected only slightly. Piedmont, except for the island of Sardinia, was a well-run state by eighteenth-century standards, but most of its rulers were devotedly Roman Catholic and some decidedly obscurantist (Doc. 1). They pursued efficiency without the aid of secularist theory. On the other hand, Parma in the 1760s, when French influence was very strong there, became a model state of the Enlightenment; and the most radical achievements of the period, both in thought and in action, were those patronized in Florence by the Grand Duke Leopold of Austria between 1765 and 1790, in Milan by his mother and brother, Maria Theresa and Joseph II, and in Naples by Charles III of Spain and his son, Ferdinand IV (later, inconsiderately, known as Ferdinand I).

It would not be difficult for any historian of any period of monarchical government to guess what were the principal fields of activity. This is, in essence, a very old story. The rulers tried to reduce the influence of the church and of the nobility, to codify laws, to foster agriculture and other industries, and to free trade by removing internal customs barriers and by abolishing out-of-date privileges of guilds and similar corporations. The princes concerned were generally working to strengthen their power and to increase their revenue. But most of them also pursued rationalization on its own account.

[6] On Protestantism, G. Spini, *Risorgimento e Protestanti* (Naples, 1956).

Milan saw the most sweeping changes. Under Maria Theresa a tax survey (*catasto*), which had been long in preparation, came into effect in 1760, and much reduced the fiscal privileges of the church and the nobility. Her other measures are described in Document 2. Joseph II, as throughout his dominions, was more ruthless than his mother. He simply abolished all the jurisdictional rights of the aristocracy, and all the old administrative organs and boundaries, and started again. He also suppressed most of the monasteries of contemplative orders, made marriage civil and dissoluble, took over education as a state concern, forbade religious processions and pilgrimages, and himself put in hand the rationalization of the church's administration. This was to carry out at one blow what in England required both the Reformation of Henry VIII and the ecclesiastical reforms of the nineteenth century. There was little left for the armies of the French Revolution to do in Milan except one very important thing, introduce representative institutions.

In Tuscany Leopold was planning to do even that when he had to leave Florence to become Emperor. His government was an example of unusually sensitive and intelligent Enlightenment, more tender towards the prejudices of his subjects than was Joseph II's. In two main respects he went further than his brother, in allowing a synod to reform the church and in promulgating an advanced criminal code. Unlike Joseph, he could and did treat his duchy as neutral, and sold off his navy. He could therefore tax more lightly.

Charles III had plans similar to those of Joseph II, but, ruling a more backward area and possessing less power himself, he could not be so drastic. His son, Ferdinand, was most conspicuous for his efforts to destroy what remained of Sicilian autonomy, but without complete success.

For all the states the church was easy game. The Counter-Reformation had still been flourishing around 1700. Louis XIV had only lately revoked the Edict of Nantes, driving out of France her remaining Protestants. After the relief of Vienna from the Turkish siege of 1683, the Austrian Habsburgs advanced rapidly south and east. The monastic orders enjoyed a last blaze of opulence and expansion in the Empire. But by the middle of the eighteenth century the avowedly Roman Catholic rulers and statesmen of Europe had turned against the Papacy, the contemplative orders and the Jesuits. Even the ecclesiastical princes of Germany gaily defied Rome, asserted the independence of the church within their states and suppressed some monasteries. The Jesuit Order, expelled from one country after another, was at length dissolved by Pope Clement XIV in 1773. Its members had to seek asylum in Protestant

Prussia and Orthodox Russia. Joseph II was the most ruthless and radical opponent of the Papacy, but all Roman Catholic princes except the popes themselves adopted policies resembling his. The prestige of the Holy See had reached its lowest point since at least the Reformation.

By the outbreak of the French Revolution the process of modernizing Italy was well under way. The economy was recovering, though not simply as a result of the reforms. The population of the peninsula went up from about twelve millions in 1700 to about eighteen in 1800, a rate of increase comparable with that of more advanced countries. There was clearly some agricultural improvement, especially an extension of maize-growing, though it is unlikely that production rose as fast as population. It was beneficial that Italy escaped involvement in the Seven Years War and the War of American Independence. The changes, however, it must be repeated, did not include the introduction of representative institutions. Such relics as survived of parliaments and city councils, for example in Sicily and Milan, were the first object of enlightened attack. Nor was there criticism of Italy's political divisions and her foreign rulers. It is hardly permissible to speak of a distinctively 'Italian Enlightenment'. There was a Neapolitan Enlightenment, undoubtedly, displaying patriotic feelings towards the Neapolitan State, and anxious to integrate Sicily into it. There was a Tuscan Enlightenment, no less loyal to the established state. Even in Milan representatives of the Enlightenment made little difficulty about co-operating with rulers based north of the Alps. The strands of eighteenth-century thought which could be woven into nationalist theory, in writings like Vico's, Shaftesbury's, Montesquieu's, Rousseau's and Herder's, were either unknown or not so applied. The general tone of the Enlightenment was positively anti-national, cosmopolitan. Since it was believed that rational solutions of universal application could be found for political, social and economic problems, there was no more need to establish nation-states than representative institutions. Existing despots would be perfectly capable of implementing the programme to the universal satisfaction (Doc. 2)[7]

[7] I have made most use of the articles of F. Valsecchi, 'Dispotismo illuminato' and B. Caizzi, 'La vita economica in Italia nel XVIII secolo' in *Nuove Questioni*, Vol. I, together with the lectures which I have been fortunate to hear in Cambridge by Professor F. Venturi of Turin on 'The Italian Enlightenment' and 'The Enlightenment'. On the church see E. E. Y. Hales, *Revolution and Papacy, 1769–1846* (London, 1960), and the books in his bibliography. There is a chapter on the Italian Enlightenment in L. Salvatorelli, *Concise History of Italy* (London, 1940). R. R. Palmer, *The Age of the Democratic Revolution*, vol. I (London, 1959) is good on Joseph II in Milan.

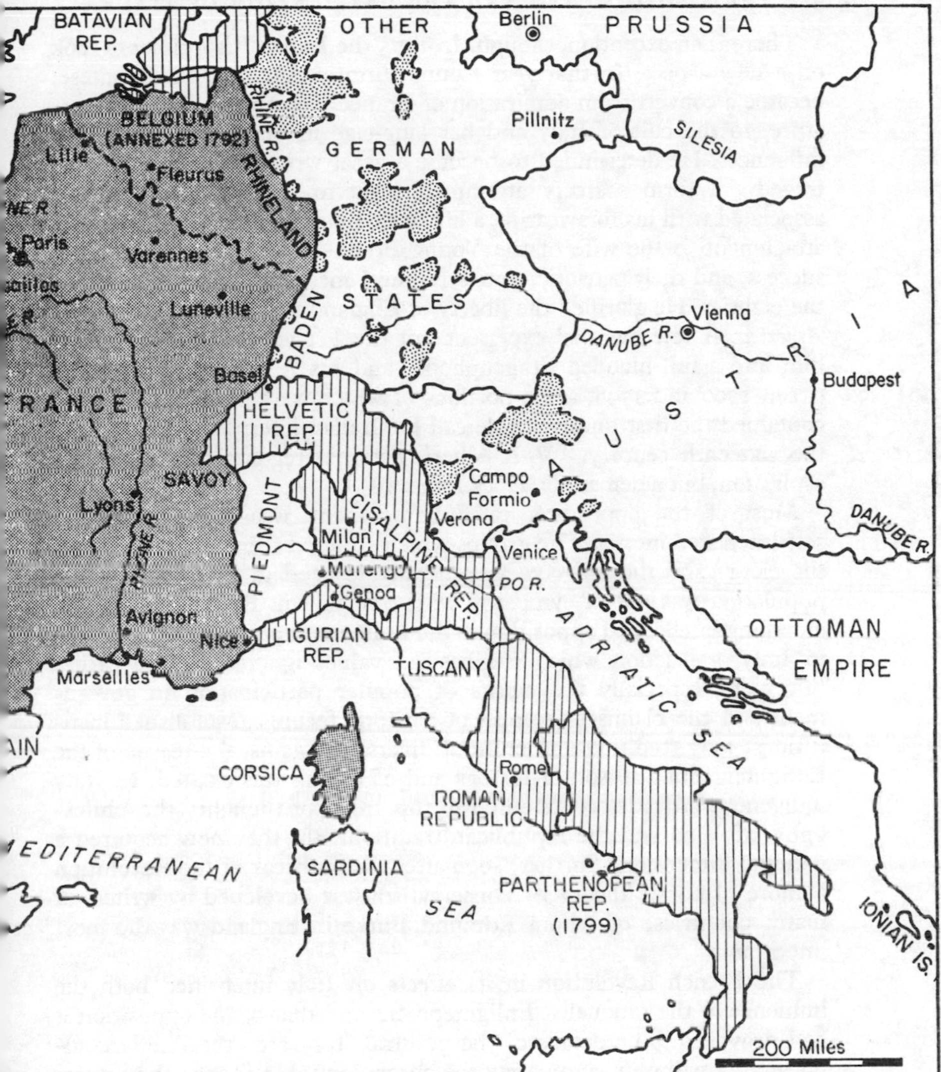

Italy and Europe, 1798

There is an exception, though. In 1775 the Italian Risorgimento took on a new aspect. In that year Count Vittorio Alfieri, a Piedmontese, became a convert from admiration of France, her philosophy and literature, to the cult of Italy and her language in opposition to French influences. He determined to become a great writer of Italian classical tragedy, a form scarcely attempted hitherto. This conversion was associated with his forswearing a life of dissipation in favour of a steady attachment to the wife of the Young Pretender. His plays had some success, and their patriotic, anti-tyrannical message some influence, in the eighties. He glorified the liberty of England and wrote *Odes to Free America*. A few months' experience of the French Revolution turned him into a full-blooded Francophobe, and his *Misogallo*, written between 1790 and 1798, some portions of which were published in 1799, contained the first unmistakable call for Italian liberty and unity since the sixteenth century. 'With Alfieri, national regeneration is not an aspiration, but a demand'[8] (Docs 1 and 3B).

Most of the opposition to Enlightenment was little more than self-interested inertia. The groups which suffered from Enlightenment, the clergy and the aristocracy, generally resisted it. The mass of the population was out of sympathy with rationalism. But there was also emerging intellectual opposition to the Enlightenment as it had appeared in Italy, a reaction which emphasized values ignored by the earlier reformers, especially the merits of popular participation in government and the claims to respect of patriotic feelings, established institutions, long tradition and cultural diversity. Against the reason of the Enlightenment a reason of history and of feeling was exalted. In Italy indigenous attitudes contributed to this trend of thought: the philosophy of Vico and the republican tradition. But they now acquired a national dimension. Further, soon after the outbreak of the Revolution a more elaborate theory of conservatism was developed by writers of many countries, of whom Edmund Burke in England was the most important.

The French Revolution in its effects on Italy intensified both the influence of the rationalist Enlightenment and that of the opposition it had provoked. The details of the political story are exceedingly complicated. I will only summarize the chronology. Until 1793 the impact of the Revolution was peaceful, but then Piedmont declared war on France. The war brought great changes to Piedmont, but did not spread to the rest of Italy until 1796. By then, as in other European countries, the Revolution had evoked some response all over the peninsula.

[8] G. Megaro, *Alfieri*, p. 128 and *passim*. V. Alfieri, *Memoirs* (ed. E. R. Vincent) (London, 1961).

Governments had at first hurried on their reforms, and then become alarmist reactionaries. Conspiracies had been uncovered, Jacobin clubs formed, and peasants had revolted. But development was much more rapid after Napoleon, as a general of the Directory, invaded northern Italy in April 1796. For one reason or another, and on one pretext or another, he had conquered the whole mainland by 1799. In that year the French were chased out again for a few months. But they returned in 1800, and by 1808 had resumed control of the whole mainland, which they retained until 1814.

On the one hand the French occupation extended the work of the Enlightened despots. Most conspicuously, the power of the Pope and of the church was further reduced. Pope Pius VI was carried off to France in 1799 and there died. His successor, Pius VII, had to be elected at Venice because of the French occupation of the mainland. He too was soon under restraint in France. In 1809 the temporal power of the Papacy was declared to be at an end. By 1814 monasteries of contemplative orders had virtually disappeared from the Italian mainland. Their lands were sold off, but in large lots, so that they were bought by persons already wealthy. In the 'plain of Bologna', for which figures happen to be available, in 1789 the church had 19 per cent of the land, nobles 55 per cent, middle-class persons 18 per cent. In 1804 the figures were 4 per cent, 50 per cent and 34 per cent.[9A] Clearly the process strengthened the Third Estate in Italy. An assault on entails, more drastic than previous rulers had made, also contributed to land redistribution and the commercialization of agriculture. Feudalism was abolished where it survived.

During the French occupation governments continued to encourage agriculture in Italy, though with the special aim of promoting the cultivation of crops which could provide substitutes for commodities rendered scarce by the British blockade of ocean trade routes. Coffee was a failure, sugar-beet a success. But they did not foster other Italian industries, because the object of French policy was to exploit Italian supplies of raw materials for the benefit of French manufactures. Hence the silk industry of Italy suffered severely. In certain respects the French were able to carry enlightened policies much further than earlier rulers, because they controlled the whole peninsula. They abolished many more impediments to trade. They built fine new roads across the Alps and the Apennines, a notable contribution to the unification of a country whose internal communications had been so poor. And they not only codified law, they standardized it over most of Italy, introducing there the French

[9A] R. Zangheri, *La proprietà terriera nella pianura bolognese (1789–1804)* (Bologna, 1961).

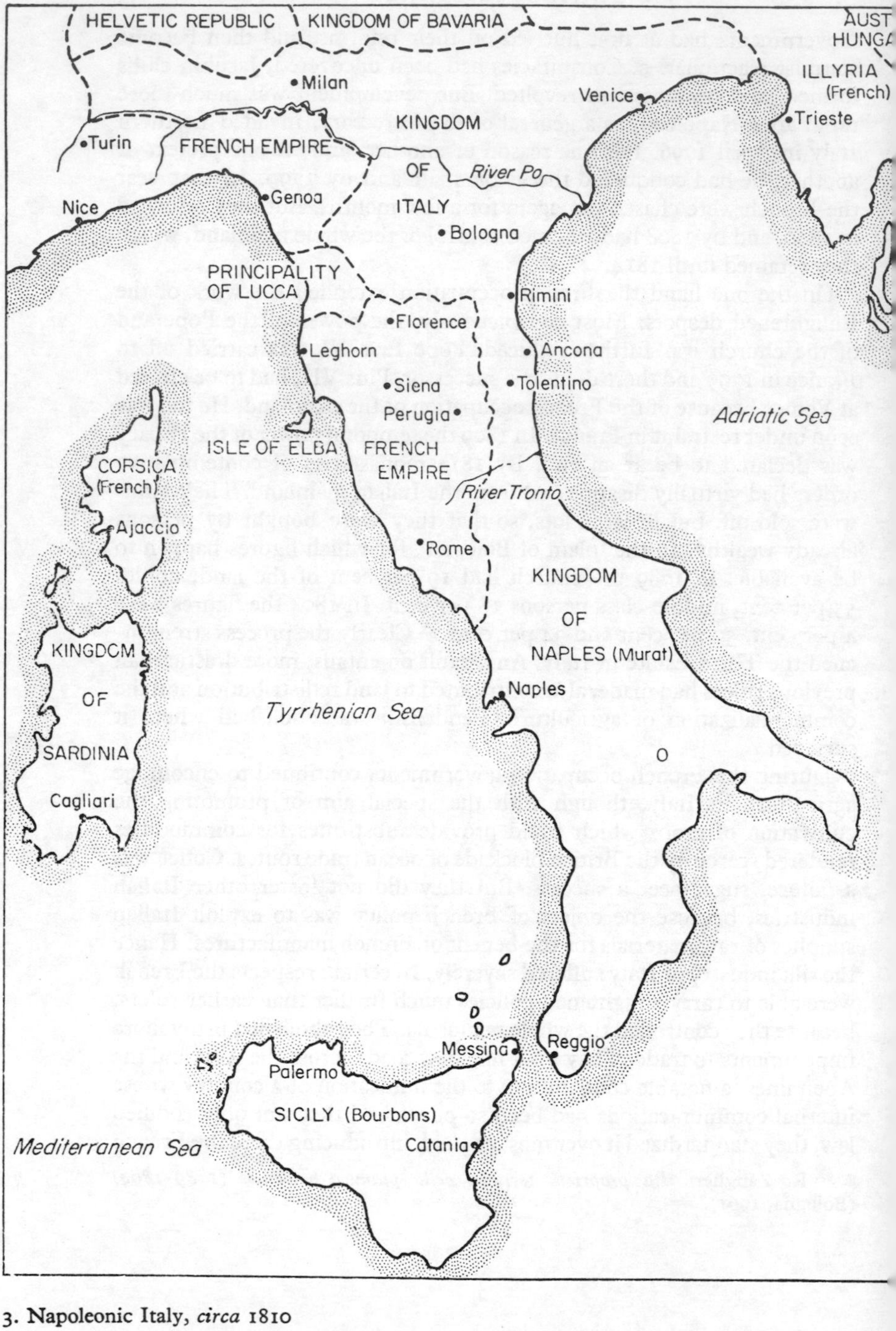

3. Napoleonic Italy, *circa* 1810

civil and commercial codes. By 1814 the work of the Enlightenment had been carried near to completion.

In two important ways, however, the French were real innovators in Italy. First, they brought representative government. By the end of 1799 every part of the mainland except Venetia, which France had presented to Austria, had had a brief experience of a republican constitution prepared under French auspices. These constitutions were moderate, modelled on the French constitution of 1795 rather than on the earlier more radical documents of the revolutionary period. But they all established representative assemblies of two chambers, with separation of powers. It was possible to obtain Italian help in framing and working these constitutions, but they varied little from state to state, and they were manifestly French in their inspiration. Then, in the second phase of French domination, all the mainland except Naples[9B] again received constitutional government of a sort, this time under monarchs.

Secondly, the French remade states with abandon, as Maps 2 and 3 show. Between 1809 and 1814 the political division of virtually the whole peninsula was simplified into three parts only, a third annexed to France, a third called the Kingdom of Italy, and a third called the Kingdom of Naples.

Much of the administrative and legislative achievement of the French was to be preserved by the regimes of the Restoration. But the Treaty of 1815 re-established a state-system in Italy similar to that of 1748–96, and all constitutional experiments were abandoned. However, nearly twenty years of French domination left more traces than the restored rulers liked. This was the greatest upheaval experienced by Italians since at least the sixteenth century. The drastic and repeated refashioning of state boundaries, culminating in the comparatively rational tripartite division, made it difficult to regard the eighteenth-century political map of the peninsula, or anything like it, as sacred. Further, the constitutional regimes had given unprecedented opportunities of political discussion and participation to the more articulate sections of Italian society. Napoleon relied on the professional classes for his main support, especially since so many of the old nobility went into exile with their sovereigns. There at once emerged a pattern which was to be recognizable throughout the next century. Napoleon wrote to the French Directory at the end of 1796:

'The cispadane republics are divided into three parties: first, the

[9B] The position in Naples is difficult to describe briefly. A constitution was supposed to be in force, another was promised, but little was actually done. See O. Connelly, *Napoleon's Satellite Kingdoms* (London, 1965).

friends of their old government; secondly, the supporters of an independent but somewhat aristocratic constitution; thirdly, the supporters of the French constitution or of pure democracy. I suppress the first, I support the second and I moderate the third.

I support the second and I moderate the third, because the second party is that of the rich proprietors and the priests, who, in the last analysis, would win over the mass of the people whom it is essential to rally round the French party.

The last party is composed of young people, of writers and of men who, as in France and in all countries, change a government and love liberty only for the sake of making a revolution.'[10]

Some representatives of the Enlightenment, like Pietro Verri, are to be found assisting in the government of these republics.[11] More important, many persons who first acquired experience of politics and administration under French occupation were prominent after 1815 in reformist, liberal and nationalist agitation (Doc. 6). Napoleon raised a large army in Italy, and officered it from a wider area of society than the armies of the *ancien régime*. The men so promoted found themselves lowered in rank after the Restoration, often in favour of aristocratic incompetents. Here was another source of discontent after 1815. The French even gave some encouragement to nationalism. In the Kingdoms of Italy and Naples the use of the Italian language was promoted, and appeals were made to Italian feeling. The King of Naples, Joachim Murat, trying to preserve a throne for himself in the wreck of the Empire in 1815, called on the people of the whole peninsula to support him and make of Italy one independent state. Though he received little assistance, his example was remembered, and until 1860 the powers had some ground for fears that members of his family might make attempts to recover a position for themselves in Italy.

Those who opposed French influence acknowledged, despite themselves, its force. In Piedmont it was the King himself who abolished the immunities of the clergy and the nobility, in order to raise enough taxation to fight the French (Doc. 5). Though the legitimate rulers of Sardinia and Sicily took refuge in these islands under English naval protection and were able to preserve there elements of the *ancien régime* which did not survive on the mainland, even here, partly to please England, the King of Naples granted a constitution to Sicily in 1812, and the aristocracy surrendered some of their feudal rights.

Anti-French feeling became more significant. In 1799 an army of

[10] *Correspondance de Napoleon* 1er, Vol. II (Paris, 1859), 207.
[11] D. A. Limoli, 'Pietro Verri', *Journal of Central European Affairs* 1958.

conservatives, with much support among the peasantry and under the leadership of Cardinal Ruffo, helped drive the French out of Naples. One of the more reluctant participants in the Republic thus overthrown, Vincenzo Cuoco, wrote an account of the Revolution which had established it, in so doing producing one of the classics of the Italian Risorgimento, glorifying Neapolitan, if not Italian, nationalism against French influences (Doc. 4). However, he later collaborated with Napoleon's puppet kings. Evidence of real Italian nationalism becomes more frequent, though it is still rare, and sometimes pro-French (Docs 3A, 3B).

An important part in the story of the period is played by secret societies. Though there is no doubt of that, it is very hard to discover what exactly they did. There were clearly by 1796 some extreme Freemasons in Italy, whose leader was Filippo Buonarroti, who were the first advocates of a united Italian republic (Doc. 3A). There were also other brands of Freemasonry and of rival societies. The best known were called the Carbonari. This name, especially as applied by opponents, covered a variety of manifestations, but had the particular connotation in many cases that Carbonarism was not, as Freemasonry commonly was, anti-Catholic. Such societies became particularly strong in Naples, partly because Murat encouraged some of them and partly because there was a long tradition of similar activity in southern Italy. There existed both pro-French and anti-French organizations, and many changed allegiance according to the situation (Doc. 7).[12]

So by 1815 Italy had passed through a social, political and constitutional revolution. Nowhere else in Europe had Enlightenment achieved such notable practical results. Nowhere else outside France and the Low Countries had the Revolution and Napoleon effected such changes. The whole story, however, is dominated by non-Italian initiatives, whether of Charles III, Leopold II, Joseph II or Napoleon. This fact obviously casts doubt on the claim that it was the Spanish domination of the sixteenth and seventeenth centuries which kept the country backward. With the overthrow of Napoleon a period began in which direct foreign influence in Italy was reactionary. It now became important that, largely under foreign auspices, there had come into being in Italy a sizable body of moderate reformers and a presumably much smaller number of radicals, and among both groups a handful of people

[12] This paragraph is worded vaguely because it seems impossible to be precise about the secret societies and at the same time accurate. See C. Francovich, 'L'azione rivoluzionaria risorgimentale e i movimenti della nazionalità in Europa prima del 1848' in *Nuove Questioni*, Vol. I; R. J. Rath, 'The Carbonari', *American Historical Review*, 1964.

who can properly be called nationalists. On the other hand, the mass of the population had shown no interest in change. In so far as they had made themselves felt, it was as supporters of the more conservative of the old regimes (Doc. 4).[13]

[13] Articles by V. E. Giuntella, 'L'esperienza rivoluzionaria' and R. Luraghi, 'Politica, economica e amministrazione nell'Italia napoleonica' in *Nuove Questioni*, Vol. I. Connelly, *Napoleon's Satellite Kingdoms*. Palmer, *Age of the Democratic Revolution*, Vol. II (London, 1964).

3

From the Restoration to 1832

The Treaty of Vienna, concluded in 1815 after the final defeat of Napoleon at Waterloo, restored the map of Italy to a state similar to that of 1748. (See Map 4.) The following were the main changes. First, the Congress which made the Treaty was not in favour of republics, and declined to restore any of the three significant Italian examples. Venetia was placed, with Lombardy, under the Austrian Empire. Genoa was given to Piedmont. Lucca became a Duchy. This reduced the number of sizable political units in Italy to nine instead of eleven. Secondly, complicated arrangements were made for the future of three of the lesser states. When the Duchess of Massa and Carrara died, her territory was to be added to the Duchy of Modena. By a supplementary agreement of 1817, when the Duchess of Parma died, the Duke of Lucca was to succeed her, and the Duchy of Lucca was to be annexed to Tuscany. So the Treaty provided for the eventual division of Italy into only seven significant parts. Massa and Carrara in fact disappeared in 1829, and Lucca, under circumstances which will be related, in 1847.

Some dynastic changes should be mentioned for clarity's sake. Modena had already descended by ordinary inheritance to an Austrian member of the old ruling family. Parma was to be ruled, during her life, by Napoleon's second wife, the daughter of the Austrian Emperor. The two technically separate kingdoms of Naples and Sicily were united as the Kingdom of the Two Sicilies, and Ferdinand IV became Ferdinand I.

Overriding all other considerations, it was the purpose of the Congress of Vienna to prevent any further attempt by France at European domination. Associated with this aim was that of suppressing the revolutionary political and social attitudes identified with French aggrandizement. As far as Italy was concerned, these ends were to be achieved by enabling Austria effectively to control the peninsula.

4. The Ten Italian States in 1815 (including San Marino)

Ruling Lombardy and Venetia herself, with members of the House of Habsburg governing Tuscany and Parma, and with an Austrian as Duke of Modena, she seemed unassailable. However, it was intended that Naples and a strengthened Piedmont should act as a counterpoise. More uncompromisingly, the powers sought to expel nationalism and liberalism, and perhaps even reformism, from the peninsula. This was the pet policy of Austria and her Chancellor, Metternich, but other countries accepted it. His plan was 'to extinguish the spirit of Italian unity and ideas about constitutions' and 'kill Italian jacobinism'. 'Italian affairs do not exist,' he said. Austria refused to have an Italian Confederation established like the German. The chief Viennese newspaper dropped its column headed *Italy* and named henceforth only the individual Italian states.[1]

Other powers, it has been said, acquiesced. The French showed no interest in Italian nationalism and liberalism, and were concerned only with frustrating what they believed to be Austria's desire to annex either Piedmont or Naples or both. The other power which took a large part in settling the future of Italy was England. The government had supported nationalist movements during the war, where convenient, but thought that the preservation of peace and of a European balance was what mattered most. Some elements of English opinion, including the Parliamentary Whigs, opposed the Treaty on the ground that it ignored Italian aspirations. But it is instructive that the aspiration which aroused most sympathy was that of the Genoese to be left independent of Piedmont. England, however, remained the country most sympathetic with liberalism, if not with nationalism, in Italy.

In the eighteenth century diplomacy and war had determined the map of Italy on the basis of dynastic interests, the balance of power and considerations of territorial compactness. To these were now added an ideological concern, recognizing the emergence of new attitudes, but only to oppose them.

It is the interpretation advanced in this Introduction that, if the peninsula was to be united in the manner of 1859–70, not only the attitudes of the people of Italy, but also those of some at least of their rulers, and those of some non-Italian peoples and rulers as well, had to change. In this chapter all these aspects will be discussed for the period down to 1832.

International developments made little difference to Italy during these years. England declined to join with the other powers in 1820 to

[1] H. A. Straus, *The Attitude of the Congress of Vienna toward Nationalism in Germany, Italy, and Poland* (New York, 1949), pp. 85–122, quotations from p. 97, 122.

suppress revolts in Spain and Italy. Her attitude of 'non-intervention' assisted the South American republics, Greece and Belgium to varying degrees of independence in the late twenties. She actually sent troops to support liberals in Portugal. But in Italy Austria, technically representing the other powers, maintained her position and stamped out liberal movements as they arose.

At the Restoration the Pope was restored as a temporal sovereign. Moreover it was a different Papacy now from that of the last days of the *ancien régime*, when a Pope had been suspected of Freemasonry and Roman Catholic rulers had assaulted the church. Her theology had become steadily more rationalist during the eighteenth century. Now emphasis was again placed on mystery, miracles, rejection of the world and repression of heretical opinion. Many rulers had become convinced that their power depended on the support of a powerful and militant church. The Jesuit order was revived in 1814. Some Italian monasteries were refounded. Though it was not possible to restore the full possessions of the church, her authority was enhanced. Austria and Tuscany refused to receive the Jesuits, but Naples and Piedmont distinguished themselves as especially devoted friends of the church. (Doc. 5).[2]

Reaction was most complete in Piedmont. She abolished the civil and commercial codes, restored the nobility to their lands and positions so far as was possible, and discouraged the use of roads the French had built[3]. In the Kingdom of the two Sicilies, by the end of 1816, the King had revoked the Sicilian constitution of 1812 and declared the two parts of his state to be administratively one.[4]

Opponents of the restored governments may be divided, for purposes of analysis, into three groups. All represented tendencies fostered by the French Revolution in some of its manifestations. There was a very small group of extremists of whom Buonarroti remained the chief almost until his death in 1837. They were likely to be republican, democratic, communist, revolutionary and unitarian (that is, in favour of unification). They were important because their faith in the perfectibility of man and the world led them to be ready to take part in underground activities and in revolts, regardless of the consequences. But they cannot be said to have been specifically Italian nationalists. They were international in their interests and in their direction. Buonarroti worked from Brussels, Geneva and Paris, and was just as concerned to

[2] Hales, *Revolution and Papacy*; W. O. Chadwick, *From Bossuet to Newman* (Cambridge, 1957).

[3] G. Guderzo, *Vie e mezzi di communicazione in Piemonte 1831–1861* (Turin. 1961); Mack Smith, *Il Risorgimento*, p. 48.

[4] L. Bulferetti, 'La Restaurazione' and R. Villari, 'L'economia degli Stati italiani dal 1815 al 1848' in *Nuove Questioni*, Vol. I.

revolutionize France as Italy. The unification of Italy was for them just another piece of rationalization. They did not give it primacy in their programme. They were Utopians of the late Enlightenment before they were nationalists (Doc. 7).[5]

Extremists collaborated to some extent with the less extreme, who are referred to as 'radicals' and roughly identifiable with the Carbonari. Their relatively mild programme was the adoption in the various Italian states of the 1812 Constitution of Spain. By contemporary standards this was a radical document. The King had surrendered his power to a legislature of one chamber. Though it had been indirectly elected, the first stage of the election had been by universal suffrage.

Then there were the 'moderates', distinguished by their advocacy of the French Constitution of 1814, under which France was governed between 1815 and 1830. This was much less radical than the Spanish Constitution of 1812. It set up two chambers, one of them hereditary and nominated; and the suffrage on which the lower chamber was elected was very restricted. In Sicily the demand was heard for the revival of the Constitution granted to the island in 1812, which was more moderate than the Spanish document of the same year but less so than the French Charter.[6]

Two important revolutionary outbreaks occurred during these years, in 1820–1 and in 1831–2. In 1820–1 the areas affected were Naples, Sicily and Piedmont. The first move came from Naples. There the Carbonari were exceptionally strong, Murat had given special encouragement to patriotic feeling, and the reaction, after showing initial moderation, had become more oppressive. Discontent in the army was the particular source of trouble. The opportunity seemed to have arrived when a revolution in Spain in January 1820, also begun by the military, extracted from the King the restoration of the 1812 Constitution. In July the same thing happened in Naples. The constitution came into force, new ministers were appointed and an assembly was elected. But difficulties quickly arose, of which the revolt of Sicily later in the same July was the most serious. It was a grave embarrassment to the Neapolitan revolutionaries, who were agreed on nothing more firmly than that Sicily must be subject to Naples. They supported the King in reconquering the island. However, the revolution there was in some respects a more fundamental movement than the one in Naples. It was at first backed by the aristocracy and also by genuine popular elements in the city of Palermo, especially the *maestranze*, artisan corporations of

[5] M. Albertini, 'Idea nazionale e ideali di unità supernazionali in Italia dal 1815 al 1918' in *Nuove Questioni*, Vol. II. Francovich, *ibid.*, Vol. I.

[6] Francovich, *op. cit.*

medieval origin, all accepting the programme of the 1812 Sicilian constitution. In Naples the discontent was an affair of the upper and middle classes.

In both provinces the revolutionaries soon began to differ among themselves. The Sicilian aristocracy became alarmed by the growing radicalism of the *maestranze*. Worse, the peasantry outside Palermo rose against them. In Naples the elected assembly and the ministers wished to move towards a more moderate constitution, such as that of France. The Sicilians were duly subjugated, but the Neapolitans achieved nothing more. For in November 1820 at the Congress of Troppau the Powers (less England) asserted the principle of intervention in the internal affairs of states, where there appeared to be a threat to European order. The King of the Two Sicilies was summoned to a further congress in January 1821 at Llubljana (or Laibach). Despite promises to his own subjects that he would do nothing of the kind, he in fact urged the powers to help him restore his position. The constitutional regime came to an end when the forces of the liberals, appealing at the last minute, like Murat, to Italian nationalism, marched into the Papal State and were defeated in March 1821 at Rieti by an Austrian army.[7]

While the Austrians were crushing the constitutionalists of Naples, a revolt occurred in Piedmont. Again there was discontent in the army, and tension between moderates and radicals. The case was complicated by the fact that moderates had some contacts with the ultimate heir to the throne, Prince Charles Albert, whose inheritance seemed to be at risk in discussions between the present rulers of Piedmont and other powers. The revolution started badly, in that the moderates tried, when it was too late, to stop it going forward. But it was successful in that it caused the King to abdicate. It happened that the immediate heir was out of Piedmont, and so Charles Albert acted as Regent. He granted the Spanish Constitution, but was at once ordered by the new King to the frontier, where he was arrested. Another Austrian army brought this revolution to an end at Novara in May 1821.[8]

In 1831 the impetus came from the July Revolution of the previous year in France. As in 1820, it looked as though the powers might be willing to allow a constitutional regime to survive. There was now thought to be a possibility of French support for Italian revolutions. Vaguely constitutionalist risings occurred in Parma, Modena and, most

[7] G. T. Romani, *The Neapolitan Revolution of 1820–1821* (Evanston, Illinois, 1950). Mack Smith, *Modern Sicily after 1713*, Ch. 38.

[8] Berkeley, *Italy in the Making, 1815 to 1846*, Ch. V. A. Omodeo, 'La leggenda di Carlo Alberto' in *Difesa del Risorgimento* (Turin, 1955).

important, the Papal State, where Bologna and the Legations were the centre of disturbance. The rulers of both Parma and Modena soon fled, although the Duke of Modena had given encouragement to the plotters in his own state, with an eye to possible aggrandizement. These revolts were not the work of the army, but of municipalities. Again the Carbonari were believed to be prominent. At the height of their success the revolutionaries controlled nearly all the Papal State. But the Austrians were called in and suppressed the revolts within two months of their outbreak.

This, however, was not the end of the story in the Papal State. The change of regime in France had produced a shift in the international situation, which was to have a slight effect on Italy in the 1830s. A conference of the powers now presented a memorandum to the Pope demanding reforms in the government of his state. He prevaricated, the Austrian troops withdrew in July, and a new revolution broke out. The Pope tried to re-establish order with his own forces, but called in the Austrians again in January 1832. They continued to occupy Bologna until 1838, and France asserted her interest by garrisoning Ancona for the same period.[9]

These revolts had achieved almost nothing. Only the memorandum to the Pope and the involvement of France could be regarded as positive results. In Sicily the *maestranze* had been abolished, and in Naples and Piedmont the reaction was intensified. Overall, Austria's control had become more direct.

Given the international situation, it was scarcely possible that any Italian liberal or patriotic movement could succeed. But the revolutions just described would hardly have produced notable results even in ideal conditions. Perhaps it made little difference to their success or failure that they were parochial, but the fact is undoubted. Sicily and Naples, it has been seen, were at odds. The revolutionary provisional government of the Romagna in 1831 declined to collaborate with that of Modena. Even Buonarroti's international conspirators were ill-co-ordinated in Italy. There was very little sign of Italian nationalism, except as a desperate resort. Much more serious was the lack of mass support for the revolutionaries. In all the areas affected the people at large, especially in the countryside, appear to have welcomed back the legitimate rulers. At least in the Papal State and Naples, loyalist groups terrorized liberals. The revolutionaries did not encourage popular participation. Ugo Foscolo, a poet who went into exile in England in 1816, had once declared that the ordinary people were too mean to take part in such a high endeavour as the Risorgimento. There was a general

[9] Berkeley, *op. cit.*, Chs VII–VIII.

fear among liberals, as elsewhere in Europe, of democracy. In any case Italy was in no condition to breed a mass movement. Even in the most advanced parts of Italy, Tuscany and the Austrian provinces, the educated classes were small, and illiteracy was very widespread. In 1871 only 16 per cent of those aged more than six were literate in the south, only 25 per cent in the centre, and less than half in the north. Italy was in this period a victim rather than a beneficiary of the Industrial Revolution. Her textile manufacturers suffered, like those of India, from the competition of Lancashire cotton. Even the straw-hat industry of Tuscany could not maintain itself against the eastern counties of England.[10] Little progress had been made towards 'literary unification' even among the upper classes. Alessandro Manzoni, having written his great novel *I Promessi Sposi* (*The Betrothed*) in Italian as he knew it in his native Lombardy, rewrote it over a period of fifteen years in true Tuscan. The original edition came out in 1825–6, the revision in 1840–2. For the lower classes Italian still did not exist.[11]

An air of fantasy hangs over the whole Italian political scene. There is bound to be some unreality associated with a movement of cultural nationalism, consciously creating art and literature for political ends. In this period the impression is enhanced by the significance of the opera and the theatre in public life. It was no doubt true in Italy, as in Spain, that the theatre was the most hopeful medium for liberal propaganda where illiteracy was general. Censorship gave few opportunities for the production of subversive plays in Italy, but there were many demonstrations and riots provoked by the singing of patriotic arias.[12] Universities, too, brought together larger numbers of people than were normally permitted to assemble. Students were particularly affected by the literary emphasis of the Risorgimento in this period, and their gatherings were liable to lead to riots.

Moreover, in many instances the confrontations were on a minute scale. The state of Modena had 400,000 inhabitants, a joke army and a tiny police force. Stendhal used little embroidery in depicting such a principality in *La Chartreuse de Parme* (1839). The Duke was well acquainted with the leaders of the little conspiracy of 1831. In one of the great histories of the Risorgimento there is a picture of the city of Modena showing the house of a principal revolutionary a few doors

[10] Eckaus, *Journal of Economic History* 1961, p. 291. C. Ronchi, *I democratici fiorentini nella rivoluzione del '48–'49* (Florence, 1962), pp. 24–32. J. H. Clapham, *Economic History of Modern Britain*, Vol. I (Cambridge, 1930), p. 183; Vol. II (Cambridge, 1932), pp. 132, 513.

[11] Mack Smith, *The Making of Italy*, pp. 70–3.

[12] I have learned much from Mr D. A. Barrass of Churchill College on these questions.

away from the ducal palace.[13] What is known as a revolution was in fact a trivial coup, far less serious than any one of a dozen English riots of the early nineteenth century, let alone the Chartist movement. What gave it its measure of importance was that the rulers as well as their opponents accepted the revolutionary myth of 1789. The petty conspiracy of 1831 in Modena caused the Duke to flee. No doubt he lacked proper means of law enforcement, but he lacked also confidence in his position. It was the weakness of the rulers, moral as well as political, which allowed these trifling movements their temporary successes.

It was not that the rulers were full-blooded tyrants. They certainly feared and disliked opposition, operated an oppressive censorship, kept many political prisoners and drove other reformers into exile. The Governor of Genoa told Mazzini that 'the government was not fond of young men of talent, the subject of whose musings was unknown to it'.[14] But their reprisals, partly through Austrian intervention, were comparatively mild. Two men each were executed in Piedmont and Naples after the revolution of 1821, another two in Modena ten years later. But the position of the rulers almost compelled them to be despots, if petty despots. They were hostages to international treaties and to Austrian domination of Italy. If they tried to introduce constitutional government, it was more than likely that they would be deposed by Austria. Probably there was insufficient support for any other regime than theirs, except for short periods when revolutionary movements took advantage of favourable turns in the international situation. Not only did the reformers lack popular support, they disagreed among themselves. Further, in so far as the rulers had a following, it was among the conservatives and clericals, whom therefore they were inclined to please. Tuscany alone remained reasonably free. The Austrian territories were the next most tolerant, and the authorities there were very unwilling to make martyrs (Doc. 6). In Piedmont, despite its clericalism and obscurantism, the administration was competent. The King of Naples was efficient in developing his merchant marine, which remained the largest of any Italian state until 1860.[15] Outside Piedmont and the Papal State the reforms of the Enlightenment and the revolutionary period, apart from those involving representative institutions, were mostly maintained, and it is easy to see enlightened inspiration still active in promoting the assimilation of Sicily's government to that of Naples, and the island of Sardinia's to that of Piedmont

[13] C. Spellanzon, *Storia del Risorgimento e dell'Unita d'Italia,* Vol. II, Milan, 1934, p. 466.

[14] Quoted in E. Kedourie, *Nationalism* (London, 1960), p. 105.

[15] *Nuove Questioni*, Vol. I, pp. 639, 780–1.

in 1832. But it was scarcely possible for any of the rulers to acquire much credit, since they were so obviously frightened puppets. By the end of 1831 five of them had called in the Austrians to put down their subjects; the King of the Two Sicilies, fortified by Papal absolution, had twice repudiated constitutions which he had sworn to uphold; the King of Sardinia had disowned a constitution granted in his name by his heir; and the Duke of Modena had betrayed the conspirators of 1831.

The Pope's position was unique. So long as it was widely assumed that the temporal power was a necessary basis for the spiritual supremacy—a view for which it was not difficult to find support in history—the inhabitants of the Papal State were doomed to be governed incompetently and illiberally. The Pope, given his worldwide claims, could hardly allow laymen to control him in his own state. He could make only limited gestures towards popular participation in government. In the memorandum of 1831 the powers recommended what they considered acceptable reforms: that the representative principle be introduced into communal and municipal affairs; that there should be established a central Junta to regulate finance, with some elected members; and that laymen should be admitted to judicial and administrative posts. But the Pope would not concede even so much as this. He set up new provincial councils, but with the following method of election: 'The communal councils were to choose electors; the electors were to draw up lists of names; from these lists of names the Papal government was to select the members of the provincial councils.'[16] Government by clergy, much more difficult to justify now that it had disappeared elsewhere in Europe and in view of the low intellectual standard of many of them, was associated with inability to keep order. It was no doubt creditable that the Pope and his cardinals were on the whole reluctant to recruit a large army, as unsuitable for an ecclesiastical state. But this restraint amounted to a loss of nerve like that of the lay sovereigns. A temporal ruler can expect to survive as such only if he behaves like one. Within the state itself, the result of the weakness of the army was that the government came to rely on semi-private bands of citizens for law-enforcement, which merely gave a licence to gang warfare. This, though, can be said for the Pope in this context. He was now always an Italian, and he commanded the widest popular respect, at least in his spiritual capacity, of any ruler in the peninsula.

Lack of realism was displayed by opponents of the established order when they ignored the international situation. It was no doubt usually necessary to ignore it to have any hope at all, but the Neapolitan revolutionaries of 1820 took an absurdly optimistic view of their chances of

[16] Berkeley, *Italy in the Making, 1815 to 1846*, p. 114.

maintaining themselves by their own unaided efforts, in neglecting to seek support among the powers.[17] In the long run, though, there was a fundamental lack of realism also in Metternich's Italian policy. As with many figures of the Restoration, he had been brought up in the free-thinking world of the late Enlightenment and privately subscribed to its views. He thought the Papal administration 'both detested and detestable'.[18] But, again like other statesmen of the time, he felt it necessary to conceal these attitudes because he believed it unsafe to act on them. To weaken the Papal State and the spiritual authority of the church would be to threaten secular authority everywhere, and in particular Austrian power in Italy. It has been usual to regard the Holy Alliance of 1815, in which most of the powers other than England declared that they would work together to maintain the *status quo* on religious as well as political grounds, as not only 'a piece of sublime mysticism and nonsense', as Castlereagh called it, and a 'loud sounding nothing', in Metternich's phrase, but also as inoperative. But in Italy, despite his private contempt for it, Metternich acted as though he accepted it. His policy was not a simple matter of pursuing Austria's interests, understood in terms of *Realpolitik*. He believed it necessary, in order to preserve her, to embrace an ideology he did not personally accept. It was the powers, of course, who had placed Austria in the position of dominating Italy in order to contain France. But Metternich had wanted and continued to desire that role for her. In deliberately setting Austrian policy against Italian nationalism, liberalism and even reformism, in maintaining satellite rulers and in preventing the development of strong Italian states, he helped to defeat his own aims in the long run. Nothing would have been more likely to prevent the unification of Italy than the establishment of a strong and independent Muratist kingdom in the southern half of the peninsula. If the nineteenth century could tolerate the continued partition of Poland, it could presumably have borne the same in Italy. But, by taking the politics of Italy under Austrian control, he was in practice treating her as an entity. Though he would not permit a proper Italian federation, he united all the rulers in subservience to Austria. In this sense the Congress of Vienna helped to give Italian nationalism its opportunity.

[17] Romani, *Neapolitan Revolution of 1820–1821*.
[18] Berkeley, *Italy in the Making, 1815 to 1846*, p. 130*n*.

Charles Albert, Mazzini and the Moderates, 1832-46

Internationally, there occurred scarcely any change affecting Italy between the 1831–2 revolutions and 1848. In all important respects the situation remained as the Congress of Vienna had left it. There is this, though, to be noticed. It is significant of developments in Italy and elsewhere that trade disputes become prominent in these years. England had a quarrel with the Neapolitan government, which came to a head in 1840, about the concession to a French company of a monopoly of sulphur mining in Sicily. This enterprise was of major importance since the island supplied up to three-quarters of the world's production of this raw material, which was then still essential to the making of sulphuric acid, itself necessary to modern industry. Palmerston succeeded in restoring freer trade.[1] In the middle forties Piedmont and Austria had a 'trade war', chiefly over salt and wine.[2]

Within Italy, the only government whose activity in this period has been considered important is that of Piedmont. At least until the accession of Charles Albert in 1831, it was notoriously clerical and unenlightened. However, in 1859–60 it was to lead Italy to unification, and in 1848 and 1849 it fought wars against Austria in support of Lombard revolts. Charles Albert was still King during these latter adventures, and granted a constitution in 1848. It is obviously a question for historians how this transformation in the role of Piedmont came about. The problem is made more difficult by the fact that Charles Albert himself began his reign, to all appearance, as a reactionary. One explanation of the change has been that he was a secret revolutionary, or at least nationalist, all his life, and that in the early part of his

[1] P. Guiral, 'L'affaire des soufres de Sicile autour de 1840', *Mélanges Pierre Renouvin: Etudes d'Histoire des Relations Internationales,* Paris, 1966. H. Acton, *The Last Bourbons of Naples* (London, 1961), pp. 113–26.

[2] Berkeley, *Italy in the Making, 1815 to 1846*, pp. 200–2, 251–3.

reign he was biding his time waiting for an opportunity to come forward as the saviour of his country. This is the kind of story which for most historical topics has been relegated to the works of novelists. But the Risorgimento is something of an exception here, since it is impossible to deny reality or importance to the secret plans of the young Louis Napoleon, and since Garibaldi's career is too romantic even for fiction. It is necessary, then, to take seriously 'the legend of Charles Albert'.

First, the historic role of Piedmont must be explained. The country had a peculiar position in international affairs, and a special tradition of foreign policy appropriate to that position. For many centuries she had been caught up in the rivalry between Valois or Bourbon and Habsburg. Playing off one against the other, changing sides at crucial moments, maintaining a sizable army to make her alliance worth having, she had emerged from almost every war stronger than she had entered it. One of her eighteenth-century kings declared that he would eat territory 'like an artichoke', piece by piece. In 1815 Piedmont duly acquired the territory of the old republic of Genoa, which more than counterbalanced the loss of a small portion of Savoy. But she failed to obtain other prizes which her King, Victor Emanuel I, was at least as anxious to win, in what became Austrian possessions or independent duchies in northern Italy. Victor Emanuel's position was the opposite of Metternich's. While the Austrian Chancellor was a man of the Enlightenment who believed it expedient to follow a policy of reaction in international relations, the King of Sardinia was a clerical obscurantist who thought it might be to his advantage to promote radical changes in the Italian state-system. At favourable moments he toyed with the idea of establishing himself as effective ruler of Italy through direct control of the north. While Austria was dominant in the peninsula, he obstructed her so far as was consistent with the restoration and preservation of his throne. He refused to co-operate in the limited federation for purposes of defence, which Metternich proposed to set up under Austrian auspices in 1815. The only kind of federation in which Victor Emanuel was interested was one which he could dominate. The Austrian Chancellor drew the parallel, already during the Vienna negotiations, between the role of Prussia in Germany and that of Piedmont in Italy. Both countries opposed the claims of Austria; both, in relation to their size, were warlike; and both were so favoured by the international alignment that there was hardly a conjunction of circumstances in which the powers could allow them to lose. Whatever may have been the case with Prussia, though, there was as yet no element of Italian nationalism in the attitude of the rulers of Piedmont, who remained French-speaking autocrats with dynastic ambitions in the eighteenth-century manner. They would use, but not surrender to, ideology. This was their strength (Doc. 5).[3]

It was most important that in 1815 Piedmont acquired Genoa. The country now became a maritime and naval power in a small way, and its rulers found themselves more involved in Italian and Mediterranean politics, and correspondingly less concerned with their borders to France and Switzerland. Further, Genoa had a totally different political tradition from that of any other part of the state. In the former republic there arose continual agitation for constitutional and liberal reform. Thus was created another significant division within an Italian state (Doc. 5). The tension between Genoa and Turin led to revolts which were as frequent and as important in the history of nineteenth-century Italy as those of Sicily against Naples and Bologna against Rome. This division became the most serious of the problems which faced the rulers of Piedmont internally, though they had also to take account of unrest in Savoy and in the island of Sardinia.

What, then, did Charles Albert do before 1846 which could be said to anticipate his actions of 1848–9? As far as international relations are concerned, it has been indicated already that to support revolutions in northern Italy which would result in the aggrandizement of Piedmont was not a departure from the state's traditional policy. However, the interventions of 1848–9 marked a decided change in Charles Albert's. For, when he had come to the throne in 1831, he had signed an alliance with Austria and had had to be restrained by Metternich from attacking newly Liberal France! Though relations with Austria, partly for economic reasons, became strained around 1840, so little idea did Charles Albert have of fighting her that his army found itself in the campaigns of 1848–9 without maps of Lombardy. He was still in 1847 planning to intervene in the Swiss civil war. Charles Albert, exceptionally among kings of Sardinia, had allowed ideology, and reactionary ideology at that, to encumber his foreign policy.

Internally, there is rather more to be said for the view that he was always a reformer. In economic matters he showed independence of Austrian influence. He modified Piedmont's Corn Law in 1834, and between 1835 and 1841 repealed the damaging restrictions on the export of raw silk. Tariffs in general were reduced, and trade treaties made with other states. Moreover, he codified some branches of the law, and he claimed to have reformed the royal council and the army in order to admit non-aristocrats to major posts.

This was a beginning. But, on the other hand, he started his reign by

[3] See L. Bulferetti, 'La Restaurazione' in *Nuove Questioni*, Vol. I

refusing an amnesty to the political prisoners of the 1821 revolution. He repressed with unusual severity a conspiracy of 1833, in which Mazzini and Garibaldi were involved. In practice he employed only nobles in his higher administration. He was a dedicated Roman Catholic who wore a hair shirt, patronized Jesuits, spent immense effort on obtaining from the Pope the honour of receiving a Papal Nuncio in Turin, and actually reintroduced the special jurisdiction of church courts over the clergy. In consequence of these policies and of the restrictive censorship which accompanied them, few reformers remained long in his state. Mazzini, a native of Genoa, had gone into exile just as Charles Albert came to the throne, and Garibaldi, from Nice, soon followed him. Gioberti, the man who became the intellectual prophet of moderate Liberal Catholicism, was forced to leave Piedmont, wrote his *Primato* in Belgium and published it first there, and later in Tuscany. Massimo d'Azeglio, a specifically anti-revolutionary aristocrat of artistic and liberal tendencies, lived for most of Charles Albert's reign outside his native state, chiefly in Milan, where under Austrian rule he could write and publish his novels, which would have been impossible in Piedmont. Cavour himself was sent to a remote castle as a suspicious character when Charles Albert succeeded, escaped to his relatives in Switzerland as soon as he could, and described Turin in this period as 'an intellectual hell'. In reality, the reforms of Charles Albert amounted to no more than a tentative return to some of the aims of the Enlightenment and the Napoleonic period, which other Italian rulers had sensibly never abandoned. But these measures were associated with a clericalism and obscurantism unique in the peninsula. Azeglio found life more agreeable even in Rome.

Part of the legend of Charles Albert derives from the strangeness of his personality. He was secretive and retiring, devout and even mystical, in Mazzini's phrase *amletico* (like Hamlet). He appeared inscrutable enough for it to be credible that he had secret plans and sorrows. It has been supposed that he took some sort of an oath in the 1820s, as the price of recognition as the heir to the throne, to have nothing to do with revolutionaries in future. It was certainly made plain to him that the Austrian Emperor had supported his rehabilitation. He was to some degree weighed down by memories of 1821 and of attempts to exclude him from the succession. But, as the historian Adolfo Omodeo concluded, his essential traits were these. He was romantic enough to conceive of himself as having a mission, and he particularly fancied himself as a soldier. He was capable of boldness, even rashness, in taking up whatever at each stage seemed to be his mission. But he had neither the ability nor the strength of character to carry a task through; and in any case he lacked realism. 'With Charles Albert the House of Savoy had passed through its romantic crisis'.[4]

The rulers of the other states are of no particular interest until the accession of Pope Pius IX in 1846. But this is the great age of Risorgimento writing. As well as of Mazzini, Gioberti and Azeglio, the period saw the production of the major creative work of Silvio Pellico, Cesare Balbo and Carlo Cattaneo. And Italian public opinion now began to move.

Among revolutionaries, the leadership and the message of Buonarroti gave place to those of Mazzini (Doc. 8). Giuseppe Mazzini was born in Genoa under Napoleonic rule in 1805. He could easily have made a success of a literary career. He was to be in demand as a critic during his long exile in England between 1837 and his death in 1872. But he decided in his twenties that his mission was political. He became involved in revolutionary activity in Genoa that was connected with the Carbonari in their more extreme manifestations and vaguely affiliated to Buonarroti's organization. In 1830 the authorities arrested him and, though he was cleared of the charges against him, he was first imprisoned and then banished. A year later he began his campaign to promote what he conceived to be a new type of revolutionary activity, with a new programme.

He saw his methods as differing from those of the Carbonari and of Buonarroti in two main respects. First, he placed less emphasis on plotting and secrecy, and more on propaganda. His *Letter to Charles Albert* of 1831 was an early attempt to use publicity in his cause. It urged the King to be true to his revolutionary past and come forward as the leader of Italian movements for freedom and nationhood. It had the effect, as Mazzini probably intended, of making public the total rift between the King and these movements. Secondly, he addressed himself not to the educated classes only, but to the people as a whole. His *Duties of Man*, a collection of political essays, was dedicated to the workingmen of Italy. It is not clear that, in the state of popular education in Italy, appeals like this had much impact. But their spirit was certainly different from that of most writings of the Risorgimento.

Not only his methods, but also his message was new. He was the first person to put forward a specifically Italian revolutionary programme. Like Buonarroti, he wanted Italy to be made one by a rising of her people, and he wanted her to be a republic. So the rising was to be directed against all the existing rulers of Italy, whether native or foreign. But he also shared the belief of the cultural nationalists that

[4] Omodeo, *Difesa del Risorgimento*, p. 235. See the whole study of which this is the concluding sentence, 'La Leggenda di Carlo Alberto'. Cf. Berkeley.

Italy had a special civilizing mission to Europe and the world. Thus he imparted a measure of political concreteness to their aspirations, while fusing them with a modified version of the old revolutionary creed. Mazzini was not an Italian nationalist purely and simply. He did not demand that Italy expand and dominate other countries. He thought that, perhaps with some minor exceptions, the boundaries of Italy were not a matter of dispute. He claimed to have as much sympathy with the national movements of other countries as with the Italian example. But his concentration was on Italy, her special problems and her individuality. This is what fundamentally separates him from Buonarroti and from the majority of the Carbonari, whether they were radical internationalists or moderate particularists and federalists.

The organization with which he proposed to replace the Carbonari and Buonarroti's international network was 'Young Italy', founded in the year of his decision to break with the older tradition, 1831. What he wrote as Instructions for its members is printed as Document 8. These points stand out. Against the moderates he is republican, not monarchical; unitarian, not federalist; revolutionary, not constitutionalist. Against the radicals he is not, or scarcely, socialist; and he prides himself on being religious, though anti-Catholic. He regards the unification of Italy as the overriding aim. And he always asserts the unity of 'Thought and Action', *Pensiero ed Azione*, his motto. For the rest of his life, he hardly deviated from working for this programme, both by plotting and by propaganda.

It is extremely difficult to assess the importance of Mazzini's influence. One complicating factor is that Mazzini, as the prophet of a new religion, still has genuine disciples and ardent admirers in Italy and even in England. In this country his views aroused much sympathy in Nonconformist circles and, in the early decades of the twentieth century, when his prophecies of a nationalist future appeared to have been realized, were widely revered. Lloyd George once asserted that the Treaty of Versailles was Mazzini's vindication. It is one of the quirks of English historiography of the Risorgimento that a Mazzinian strand runs through it. Bolton King wrote the prophet's *Life*, published in 1902, and had edited some of his essays. G. O. Griffith's *Mazzini: Prophet of Modern Europe* (1932) is hagiography. More recently, Mack Smith has written a powerful apology for Mazzini, and Hales, while rejecting his religion, takes it exceedingly seriously.[5] On the other hand, E. J. Hobsbawm's *Age of Revolution* misses no opportunity to slight Mazzini and minimize his influence, picturing the half-century before

[5] Mack Smith's piece is 'An Idealist in Action', *Times Literary Supplement* 1955 (21 January). Hales, *Mazzini and the Secret Societies.*

1848 as little more than a prelude to the supposedly socialist, even Marxist, upheaval of 1848.[6]

Mazzini's impact outside Italy was no doubt greatest after his country had been unified, and as his doctrines seemed to be triumphing in the rest of Europe. Not only in England, but in other European countries and also outside Europe, he was regarded as a hero and a prophet. Gandhi, trying to inspire his Indian compatriots in Africa with national feeling, praised his example.[7] But the question that is important for this book is: what influence did he exert in Italy and outside in the years before unification?

Undoubtedly, his affirmation of Italian nationalism in the early thirties was important. It was known to intellectual, reformist and revolutionary circles all over the peninsula. Probably no more than a few hundred copies of each of his earlier writings were sold. It is hard to believe, as he claimed, that there were over 50,000 persons 'affiliated' to Young Italy. But he evidently gave new life to the extremist movement, whether supposedly Carbonaro or not. In the 1840s one of his journals approached a circulation of 2000. Just after 1848, another paper of his came near selling 4000.[8] The chronology of his influence is obscure. But it is plain from the fact that he was made a Triumvir of the Roman Republic in 1848–9 that he was then accepted as one of the leaders of the Italian movement. It would seem that he was most widely followed and respected in the years immediately following his work in Rome and that, as the support of Piedmont enhanced the prestige of the moderates in the course of the 1850s, his influence receded.

That influence, however, was more than literary. There was action as well as thought (and writing). Even if he greatly exaggerated the number of people involved in Young Italy—as he certainly rated absurdly highly the appeal of the later Young Europe, with its mere handful of members—he proved able, like Buonarroti and the Carbonari, to induce a few bold spirits to take up arms in the conviction that they would thereby bring the whole country out in revolution. His plots were ludicrously unpractical so far as that expectation was concerned. On one occasion at least, the representatives of the Italian people in the vicinity set on the Mazzinians as soon as they ventured to set foot on land. But these attempts always drew attention to the fact that there was a nationalist creed for which some were ready to die. Further, there were

[6] E.g. pp. 120, 132 of the original edition of 1962.

[7] D. Beales, 'Mazzini and Revolutionary Nationalism' in ed. D. Thomson, *Political Ideas* (London, 1966).

[8] L. Balestrieri, 'Dati sulla tiratura e la diffusione dei giornali mazziniani' *Rassegna storica del Risorgimento* 1950.

moments when a tiny group of enthusiasts could exploit a revolutionary situation with far-ranging results. The Palermo revolution of 1848, the first of all the revolutions of that year, would probably never have materialized but for such judicious encouragement. In 1860 Mazzinians helped to promote the revolt in Sicily which Garibaldi was induced to assist with his Thousand, among whom also were some devotees of the prophet. In general, the threat even of minor outbreaks, coupled with the fear of assassination, to which Mazzini's attitude was considered ambivalent, exerted a continual pressure on the rulers of the Italian states. Knowing how unstable their regimes were, they had reason to be sensitive to the most trivial threats. This type of plotting, though, was never confined to Mazzinians. Other brands of revolutionary activity persisted. By the disputes that raged between the different sects, of course, the movement gained only discredit.

In the last analysis, however, it was not the risings he inspired, the societies he formed, or the newspapers and pamphlets he wrote and edited, which were his greatest contribution. Nor was it his thought, which now seems every bit as much like sublime mysticism and nonsense as the ideas behind the Holy Alliance, and which even in the 1830s and 1840s won few full-blooded adherents. What mattered was the personality behind, and taken in conjunction with, these activities and this creed. No one ever doubted his dedication to his cause, shown in the personal sacrifices he made for it, of money, comfort and literary reputation. He risked his life repeatedly in visits to Italy. And no one escaped the spell of his character. This gentle, courteous, guitar-playing aesthete not only captivated women by the hundred—including many English middle-class wives, like Mrs Carlyle—but he also won for a time the devotion of many male Italian patriots. The infatuation was usually not lasting: very few indeed, even among the genuine revolutionaries, followed him wholeheartedly for long. But a great many, like Garibaldi, were introduced by him to revolutionary activity. His significance as a symbol, as Italy incarnate, was immense. In his lifetime he was incomparably more effective than Marx.

Mazzini was by the forties the only Italian revolutionary leader of significance. The moderate movement within the Risorgimento was more diversified, and no doubt had a wider appeal, It is usual to list the five great names, Pellico, Gioberti, Balbo, Azeglio and Cattaneo, and discuss their writings. There seems no escape from this historiographical tradition. But it is necessary also to take into account more general developments.

Of the five, Pellico's work came first. He was a Piedmontese who was involved in liberal journalism in the comparatively free atmosphere of

Milan in the years before 1820, and who also became a Carbonaro. He was arrested and spent most of the next decade in the Spielberg in Moravia, regarded as the worst of Austrian prisons. In 1832 he published an account of his experiences in captivity, called *Le mie prigioni* (My Prisons). The book was, deliberately, very moderate in tone. During his imprisonment Pellico had become a most devout Catholic, and he was at great pains to give credit wherever possible to his captors. He also denounced revolutionary activities. As a result the Piedmontese censors saw nothing objectionable in the book, and allowed it to appear in the kindgom of Charles Albert. But in the event *Le mie prigioni* had an enormous impact not only as a testimony to Christian resignation but also as a condemnation of a system which subjected good men who had committed comparatively slight offences to years of lingering cruelty. The book went through numerous editions in a few years, was translated into several languages and aroused sympathy for the author and other persecuted Italians all over the world. It was immensely damaging to the reputation of Austria for civilized and enlightened rule.[9]

Le mie prigioni was not explicitly, and was only half-intentionally, a political tract. But it foreshadows the moderate movement of the forties, as does the work of Manzoni. Both combined strict Catholicism and a total rejection of violent methods with affirmations of Italian distinctness and criticisms of foreign rule. It is with Gioberti that a more specific political programme is mapped out for moderate patriots. He published his *Del primato morale e civile degli italiani* ('Of the Moral and Civil Primacy of the Italians') in 1843. Historians, following contemporaries, have scoffed at the fantasies of Mazzini's thought and the unpracticality of his conspiracies. But nothing could be more absurd and unrealistic than the *Primato*. Moderates as well as revolutionaries had a stake in cloud-cuckoo-land. Gioberti's is in large parts a long-winded, frothy, silly book. He fortunately made it easy for its quality to be savoured by providing a summary of his argument serving also as a table of contents, which is printed as Document 9. The reader will find it a choice example of philosophical Idealism at its most nonsensical.

In relation to Italy's present situation, Gioberti's essential claim was that the Papacy and Roman Catholicism were the glories of Italy and must lead her national revival. He advocated a federation of Italian states under the presidency of the Pope. He rejected revolutionary means, he saw no prospect of unification and, in order to improve his book's chances of satisfying the censors, said nothing about expelling the Austrians. Fatuous though much of the *Primato* is, its influence was

[9] Mack Smith, *The Making of Italy*, pp. 66, 70. There is a modern English edition: *My Prisons* (London, 1963), translated by I. G. Capaldi.

very great. An edition of 5000 was soon printed at Florence. The appeal of its immediate programme is not hard to understand. It chimed in with the half-formed assumptions of many pious Italians. Moreover, Liberal Catholicism was flourishing in Belgium during the period of Gioberti's exile there, giving hope to sympathizers in Italy. In general, the glorification of Catholicism has to be set in the context of a period when grown Englishmen were persuaded by the arguments of Pugin's *Contrasts* and the *Tracts for the Times*.[10]

Two books followed quickly in direct response to Gioberti's: Cesare Balbo's *Delle speranze d'Italia* ('Of the Aspirations of Italy') of 1844; and Massimo d'Azeglio's *Degli ultimi casi di Romagna* ('Of Recent Events in the Romagna') of 1846. Both were anti-revolutionary and displayed no faith in the ideal of unification. But both criticized the Liberal Catholic position of Gioberti and stressed instead the role Piedmont might play as leader of Italy. Unlike Gioberti, Balbo dared to say that it was necessary to displace the Austrians. He also advocated a customs union of Italian states. Azeglio's book had the more limited aim of revealing how unpopular and reactionary the Papal Government was, through an account of disturbances in the Romagna. Neither Balbo nor Azeglio, however, could suggest any more effective mode of action than fostering a liberal Italian public opinion. Although both authors were Piedmontese and cast Piedmont for the principal role in the Italian national movement, their books could not be published under Charles Albert's rule. They appeared abroad or in Florence.[11]

It is striking how close were the personal connections between the main writers of the moderate movement. Manzoni was a grandson of Beccaria, Azeglio married Manzoni's daughter, Azeglio and Balbo were cousins, Pellico was a friend of Balbo's. Gioberti dedicated his book to Pellico, Balbo his to Gioberti, Azeglio his to Balbo. In 1848–9 Balbo, Gioberti and Azeglio were all to be Prime Ministers of Piedmont. This was a very small circle of Piedmontese and Lombard aristocrats and upper middle class, which it is tempting to dismiss as a mutual admiration society presuming to instruct Italians as a whole. But it was truly important, both because it could play a special part in Piedmontese politics when the thaw came and because there was little competition from other parts of the peninsula to provide alternative moderate leadership.

[10] Berkeley, *Italy in the Making, 1815 to 1846*, esp. Ch. XI. See Omodeo, 'Gioberti e la sua evoluzione politica' in *Difesa del Risorgimento*.

[11] Berkeley, *op. cit.*, Chs XII–XIII. R. Marshall, *Massimo d'Azeglio* (London, 1966). E. R. Vincent published a translation of *I miei ricordi* as *Things I Remember* in 1966.

There was, however, some competition. In Lombardy and in Tuscany—still, despite Austrian rule over the first and influence in the second, the freest areas of Italy—moderate groups opposed not only Mazzinianism but also liberal Catholicism and the Piedmontese party. The severity of repression and censorship in both provinces varied from time to time, but was seldom great, and many patriotic activities were carried on more or less openly. This was not a novelty of the period after 1832. Pellico had been one of the principals in a short-lived journal, *Il Conciliatore*, based on Milan, which in 1818 and 1819 had sought to provide a forum for the whole of Italy. The Austrians suppressed it, and in the 1820s such activity went underground (Doc. 6). But increasingly in the thirties and forties 'pan-Italian' movements came into the open again. In Tuscany the Grand Duke was very easy-going and paid little more than token attention to the Austrians' complaints at the criticism of their government in books and journals published in Florence. He and his ministers encouraged scientific academies, agricultural improvement and Free Trade, and believed that their best policy was to ignore subversive activities so far as possible. They were successful for a long time, in that many Tuscans who were sympathetic with Mazzini's aims abominated his methods, thinking it absurd to work to overthrow for the sake of a highly unrealistic vision the only Italian ruler who showed himself to be a reformer.[12]

Among the causes promoted by moderate reformers, conscious in varying degrees of playing a part in reviving Italy, were these. They founded agricultural societies, Lancaster schools, savings-banks, children's homes, insurance societies and learned periodicals. They promoted land reclamation, railways and gas-lighting. Individuals developed the cheese industry of Gorgonzola and the first Italian brewery. Baron Ricasoli established the reputation of the Chianti vineyards at Brolio. Great attention was paid, with some success, to reviving the silk textile industry of northern Italy. The removal of internal customs barriers, some of which had been restored in 1815, was canvassed, as was the lowering of tariffs. The Austrian government was sympathetic to economic liberalism. It was in Lombard periodicals that the campaign was carried on to induce Charles Albert to modify the Corn Law and abandon the silk embargo of Piedmont. 'Victorianism' emerges as a European phenomenon.[13]

Perhaps the most important activities for the history of the nationalist

[12] For Tuscany Ronchi, *I democratici fiorentini*, esp. Ch. II; Hancock, *Ricasoli*, early Chs; Mack Smith, *The Making of Italy*, pp. 56–63.

[13] For Lombardy K. R. Greenfield, *Economics and Liberalism in the Risorgimento* (Baltimore, 1934).

movement were the running of journals and the calling of scientific congresses. In both cases the organizers tried to cater for the whole of Italy, while ignoring or minimizing the connexions that existed between Italy and German-speaking countries. It is significant that they often had difficulty in obtaining information about southern Italy, which was in reality much less closely associated with the plain of Lombardy than Austria was. Carlo Cattaneo made his name as editor of one of the most famous of these journals, *Il Politecnico*, founded in 1839. His interests were very wide, but perhaps he was especially strong as an economist. His political attitude was that Italy could not be satisfactorily united under one administration, that some measure of federalism was alone appropriate to so diverse and divided a country. He differed from the Piedmontese moderates in putting liberty before independence, and in being a republican and a democrat. The all-Italian scientific congresses also began in 1839, and were held annually thereafter in different Italian cities.[14]

Gradually Charles Albert allowed these influences to spread into Piedmont, though he made necessary even more subterfuges than did other rulers. It was a landmark when Cavour founded a whist club there in 1841. An agricultural Association followed in 1842. The scientific congresses were permitted to meet in Piedmont in 1840 and 1846. But not until 1847 could an avowedly political and nationally-minded periodical be founded there, again with the collaboration of Cavour, under the title *Il Risorgimento*.[15]

There seemed at this moment to be real substance in Azeglio's hopes that the development of public opinion could free Italy. Under whatever guise people met, liberal and national aspirations were discussed. Short of violent repression, which the governments were reluctant to risk, public opinion seemed certain to exercise an irresistible influence on the petty regimes of Italy. This was the great period of the Risorgimento, of the national movement proper.

[14] Mack Smith, *The Making of Italy*, pp. 56, 92–100. Greenfield, *Economics and Liberalism*.

[15] A. J. Whyte, *The Early Life and Letters of Cavour* (Oxford, 1925), pp. 252–3, Chs XI–XII.

5

The Forty-Eight

To give anything approaching a complete account of the 1848 revolutions in Italy would be a vast undertaking. Cesare Spellanzon's large-scale history of the Risorgimento spends five huge volumes on 1846–9. Even Berkeley wrote two on 1846–8. I am going to limit narrative to a minimum, and concentrate on the origins, the general characteristics and the consequences of the revolutions.

The most convenient starting-point, and a date of real significance, is the election of Pius IX as Pope in June 1846. He at once amnestied many political prisoners, and introduced various reforms in the government of the Papal State, providing for some lay participation. These actions made people all over Italy believe that the Pope was implementing the programme laid down for him by Gioberti. Pius IX certainly had some sympathy with his views.[1]

Once one state began to reform, in the climate of opinion, the others had to follow. Piedmont and Tuscany had already moved forward some distance by the end of 1847, for example in freeing the press; and in November of that year the rulers of those states made an agreement with the Pope on the basis of a customs-union between the three countries. Though the agreement was only in principle, and got no further, it was considered a tremendous advance. Agitation for reform in Austrian territory, and in the lesser states contiguous with it, as well as in the Kingdom of the Two Sicilies, intensified. Metternich became so conscious of the weakness of Austria's position in the new situation that he considered it necessary, in order to preserve a measure of control over the Duchies of Parma and Modena and over the Papal State, to make special treaties of alliance with the first two, going beyond the Treaty of Vienna, and to reinforce the Ferrara garrison in order to

[1] Hales, *Pio Nono*.

overawe the Pope. Pius protested at this, and was able to compel withdrawal.[2]

A trivial story, that of the Duchy of Lucca, illustrates the state of unrest in northern and central Italy. The Duke of Lucca tired, during the course of 1847, of waiting for the Duchess of Parma to die. Partly for personal reasons connected with his finances, but partly also because of reforming demands made upon him by the inhabitants of his Duchy, the Duke instructed his chief minister, Baron Ward, who had started his career as a groom in Yorkshire, to arrange the sale of his rights over his state, and the immediate transfer of the territory to Tuscany, with a small residue to himself and some compensation to Modena. This arrangement provoked discontent in the areas arbitrarily allocated, and a tiny war between Tuscany and Modena over the spoils. These incidents illustrate that the rulers' position was weakened and reformist feeling widespread, but also that state rivalries and particularism remained important (Doc. 10).[3]

In the background of the general movement of discontent in Italy and in the rest of Europe was the economic crisis caused by the failure of the harvest in 1847. The threat of starvation was close enough to make rioting endemic throughout the Continent.

Up to the end of 1847, though, nothing that could properly be called a revolution had taken place in any of the Italian states, and the only serious rising to have occurred in Europe was a peasants' revolt of 1846 in Galicia, an Austrian province. On the other hand, all over Italy attempts to celebrate the first anniversary of Pius IX's accession had caused disturbance and alarm. At the very beginning of 1848 a 'tobacco strike' was called by the opponents of Austrian rule in Lombardy. The idea recalled the Boston Tea Party. Italians were asked to refrain from smoking cigars, in order to deprive the Austrian revenue of the tobacco tax. During the 'strike' there were riots and casualties. But the first actual revolution of 1848, not only in Italy but in the whole of Europe, was that of January 12, 1848, in Palermo. It was as broad a protest against Neapolitan government as that of 1820, with perhaps a slightly larger admixture of Italian nationalism. Practically all classes united to seize control of the city, whether for patriotic reasons or with a view to exploiting the confusion for private advantage. The King of the Two Sicilies asked Austria to assist him against the rebels. Metternich had to reply that she could not. So a Constitution was granted to the Kingdom late in January (Doc. 12).

[2] Berkeley, *Italy in the Making, June 1846 to January 1848*, Chs XIV–XV.

[3] *Ibid.* pp. 242–6, 341–3. J. Myers, *Baron Ward and the Dukes of Parma* (London, 1938).

With Austria so weak, no Italian ruler could stand against the movement of opinion, except the Dukes of Modena and Parma, both directly protected by Austrian troops. In February the Grand Duke of Tuscany and the King of Sardinia promised constitutions. In March the Pope himself followed suit. In the same month Vienna itself rose, Metternich went into exile, and the Emperor granted constitutions. Immediately, revolts in Venice, under Daniele Manin, and in Milan, where Cattaneo was prominent, drove out Austrian troops. The rulers of Parma and Modena now had to leave their states. Before the end of March, forced on by the enthusiasm of his subjects, and especially by discontent in Genoa, Charles Albert was at war with Austria in support of the revolts in Lombardy and Venetia. Tuscany and Naples gave at least token support to Piedmont. For a few weeks during the summer of 1848 Lombardy, Venetia, Modena and Parma were fused into one state with Piedmont.

In July, however, Marshal Radetzky, the Austrian commander in Italy, inflicted a defeat on the Piedmontese at Custoza, and in August Charles Albert signed an armistice, ceding back all the territories which had just joined Piedmont, as it had been stated, 'irrevocably'. With the recovery of Austria, it was only a question of time before all the Italian revolutions were suppressed.

What happened in five of the provinces should be briefly recounted. First, Venice reverted, after the defeat of Piedmont, to a republic, and resisted Austrian troops and sailors until August 1849. Tuscany, secondly, became too radical for the Grand Duke, and he abandoned it, in February 1849. The 'democratic' or republican government proved extremely weak, and a combination of aristocratic moderates and Austrian troops restored the Grand Duke in April. Thirdly, the Pope's affair with liberalism came to an end in April 1848, when he refused to join Piedmont in the war against Austria. He tried for several months longer to work with his new constitutional government, but gave up the attempt in November and left Rome. In February 1849 a republic was declared there, and became a refuge for radicals from all over Italy. Mazzini was one of its triumvirs, Garibaldi commanded its defenders. It held out until July 1849, when the combined forces of France and Austria restored the Pope. Fourthly, a quite different pattern appeared in Naples: the king re-established his position without foreign intervention. He then conquered Sicily. Fifthly, Piedmont's government moved to the Left like those of Tuscany and Rome, and Charles Albert found it necessary to declare war on Austria again in March 1849. He was at once conclusively defeated at Novara, abdicated, and left his son Victor Emanuel II to restore the situation.

(Docs. 11–13.) Much more will be said of subsequent Piedmontese developments later.

With regard to the causes of the revolutions, they were very various. In this connexion all factors do seem to work together to promote the Risorgimento, as the myth requires. The events cannot be explained without taking into account the temporary paralysis of France as well as of Austria in this year of general revolution. The economic situation made some sort of popular rising likely. The Liberal Catholic movement was essential to the story, inducing many persons who might have been expected to be conservatives to take part in reformist and liberal, if not revolutionary, activities. The kind of opinion to which Azeglio appealed was important, and so was the Mazzinian sector. The expansionist tradition of Piedmont worked together with the democratic impulse of Genoa and Milan. The separatism of Sicily started the chain of revolutions.

As to the general characteristics of the revolutions, there was, on the one hand, much more impressive support shown for movements of political protest than ever before in Italy. Some collaboration proved possible in most states between moderates and radicals. In the towns the revolutionaries commanded real popular support at times. The intervention of Charles Albert, however dubious his motives, was the first active assistance given by an established Italian ruler to anti-Austrian revolutionaries. A measure of inter-state co-operation was achieved. The Kingdom of North Italy, created in the summer of 1848, was an important precedent for later changes. The Roman Republic was pan-Italian.

On the other hand, the variety of causes and motives displayed itself in fatal disputes, distrust and divisions. The Romagna on this occasion remained loyal to the Pope in order to preserve its opposition to the City of Rome. The Austrians were able to exploit the fact that many inhabitants of the Veneto wished it to be distinct from Venice. Sicily rose against Naples (Doc. 12). Tuscany made sure that the first territory she invaded during the war of 1848 was the area recently disputed with Modena. Even during the republican phase, Tuscans and Romans would not unite.

There were disputes between parties too. Cattaneo would not recognize, and Manin was very reluctant to accept, the leadership of the King of Sardinia. Charles Albert declined to use the volunteers sent him from other states, thinking it improper to depend on other than regular soldiers. He also refused to work with revolutionaries unless they would declare themselves supporters of the Piedmontese ruling house. Suspicion of his motives was widespread, though perhaps less so than was justified.

In general, the peasantry, except in Sicily, remained supporters of the old regimes and assisted their restoration. The revolutionaries did not distinguish themselves for good sense. Few of them seemed to realize how fortunate the circumstances were which had forced the rulers to make concessions or abandon their states. Little appreciation was shown of problems of power-politics.

During the revolutions it was proved that the Risorgimento had now progressed a long way. Probably most politically articulate Italians had expressed feelings of criticism towards their rulers and the existing regimes. Many had shown themselves liberal, and some nationalists. But in the fifties the whole experience of 1848–9 seemed to have left little trace. If anything, it had resulted in more oppression by Austria and her satellites than previously. At this second restoration no change was made in the political map of Italy, and the only state in which any of the achievements of 1848 survived was Piedmont, which retained her constitution and a measure of freedom.

Moreover, the events of 1848–9 had totally discredited Liberal Catholicism. It had been demonstrated that the Pope could not be a constitutional sovereign of the Papal State, since this was incompatible with his rule over the worldwide Roman Catholic Church. His refusal to join in the war of liberation, while well justified on religious grounds, disqualified him as an effective temporal ruler. Gioberti himself abandoned the position he had adopted in the *Primato*, and turned to the Piedmontese and their king, or to the French Republic set up in 1848, for a saviour for Italy. His recantation appeared as *Il Rinnovamento civile d'Italia* ('The renewal of Italian public life') in 1851. The Pope himself made no further gesture towards liberalism and constitutionalism. This is not to say that belief in the possibility that the Pope might lead Italy to freedom had been unimportant in 1846–8. On the contrary. But after 1849 few people retained it.

The experience of 1848–9 had also discredited another hitherto moderate influence, the Grand Duke of Tuscany. Restored with the aid of Austrian troops, who remained in occupation of the Duchy until 1855, he was reduced to the status of a mere Austrian puppet like the other central Italian rulers.

Austria occupied not only Tuscany, but also the Duchies of Parma and Modena and the Romagna, in these cases right down to 1859. Further, a state of siege was imposed on Lombardy and Venetia until 1857. Her hegemony was now much more explicitly maintained by force of arms, and such reputation as she had possessed for enlightenment virtually disappeared.[4]

[4] Berkeley's volumes, so far as they go, are the best account of the '48 in English. See also Acton, *The Last Bourbons of Naples*, Chs IX–XIII; Mack

In summary, for all the importance of the '48 revolutions in the history of the Risorgimento, they had a mainly negative significance for the unification of Italy. The most important single lesson to be derived from their failure was that the development of the national movement counted for very little in the scales against changes in the international situation. It was only when the Austrian cat was distracted that the Italian mice could play.

Smith, *Modern Sicily after 1713*, Ch. 45; A. J. P. Taylor, *The Italian Problem in European Diplomacy, 1847–1849* (Manchester, 1934); G. M. Trevelyan, *Manin and the Venetian Revolution of 1848* (London, 1923).

The Italian literature is enormous. Most important is Spellanzon, *Storia del Risorgimento*, Vols III–VII. Candeloro's Volume III is devoted to the years 1846 to 1849. See bibliography in *Nuove Questioni*, Vol. I, pp. 708–17.

6

The Transformation of Piedmont 1849-59

There were Italians who did not accept the lessons of 1848–9 as conclusive, who continued to hope in Liberal Catholicism, to share Mazzini's faith in the prospects of a general Italian insurrection, or even to trust in the Grand Duke of Tuscany. But, for those who could bring themselves to see it, the most encouraging aspect of the Italian situation after 1849 was the position of Piedmont. The essential facts were that she retained her constitution and therefore a measure of freedom, and that her dynasty remained independent of Austria.

It was difficult for contemporaries to give these facts their full significance, because the behaviour of Charles Albert and, to a lesser extent, of his successor was equivocal. Charles Albert had been most reluctant to grant the constitution. His support of Lombard and Venetian revolutionaries had been less than wholehearted—tainted by the motive of aggrandizement and marred by military inefficiency. He seemed to have become a constitutionalist and a nationalist merely in order to preserve his throne. Apart from the question of his motives, his policy had been as unrealistic as those of Gioberti and Mazzini. He had proclaimed: *Italia farà da sé* ('Italy will manage by herself'). This attitude looked preposterous after the experience of 1848–9. The moment the Austrians recovered themselves, the Italian revolutionaries, even when supported by the armies of Piedmont, were lost. While patriots were now bound to value more highly than hitherto the only military force of any consequence in Italy which had opposed itself to Austria, they were also compelled to recognize that it would need an ally to be in a position to defeat her.

Charles Albert deserved to be distrusted. But it is fair to emphasize that the position of Piedmont was unavoidably ambiguous. This is well illustrated in the negotiations and political manoeuvres which led to the maintenance of the constitution after the defeat at Novara in 1849.

aly at the Beginning of 1859

When Charles Albert abdicated, it was presumably because his credit as a ruler and general had been totally destroyed by this second defeat. Perhaps an alternative existed: the constitution might have been suspended, and Austrian troops called in to maintain the regime. But the other powers would have disliked that course, and might have forbidden it. As in 1821, abdication alone gave an opportunity for the dynasty to restore its position.

Victor Emanuel was left to conduct the necessary armistice negotiations with Radetzky. The legend was propagated in the following years that Victor Emanuel's firmness and courage preserved the constitution against Austrian demands that it be revoked. This story, though plausible enough in the light of Austria's attitude earlier and later in the century, is certainly untrue.

It was a unique moment. Austria herself was supposed to be a constitutional state. Much of Italy was under republican government. Piedmont's constitution, as will be seen later, was very moderate, much more acceptable to Austria and to other powers than those of the republics. It remained likely that, if Austria had tried to destroy the Piedmontese constitution, France, still under republican government, would have intervened, with Britain's acquiescence, to save it. As Radetzky saw the situation, it was in the interests of Austria to support Victor Emanuel and to make things as easy for him as possible, in order to help him defeat the Piedmontese radicals. The dynasty's position was obviously precarious. Genoa was in revolt. The opposition, commanding a majority, demanded a renewal of the war. Radetzky therefore mitigated the terms of the armistice as much as he dared, and more than the authorities at Vienna were prepared to accept.

Victor Emanuel's own attitude to the constitution is hard to determine. His remarks were seldom measured. He spoke of the constitution with disrespect, but he also took credit for saving it. As for Radetzky, he had no particular interest in the question. But their precise views are unimportant. For they did not consider the fate of the constitution on its own merits, in isolation. They saw it as a factor in a complex political situation. They were both realists, and this was the essential reason why they wished the constitution to survive. Radetzky did not in fact ask for its abrogation. Victor Emanuel did not have to struggle to defend it. The point was that international considerations required that this buffer-state should be independent, and, as things were, it seemed that she could stay independent only if she retained her constitution. Since Austria could not risk occupying Piedmont, the next best course was for her to assist Victor Emanuel to preserve the moderate constitution. Whether Victor Emanuel liked the constitution or not, his only hope of remaining King was to uphold it. The armistice, therefore, can be represented as a plot by the rulers of Austria and Piedmont against radical republicanism in Piedmont and the rest of Italy.

Radetzky, however, could not control the authorities in Vienna. During the negotiations to convert the armistice into a peace, additional demands were made on Piedmont, which would have made Victor Emanuel's task more difficult still, and would have required him to repeal by royal decree laws passed by the country's Parliament. In refusing to do so, and enlisting sufficient support from other powers to cause Austria to climb down, the King in a sense saved the Constitution. On one point, though, he did act unconstitutionally. He ratified the treaty although it contained an indemnity clause and a clause renouncing Sardinia's claim to the territories annexed in 1848. Under the Constitution any transfer of territory and any financial burden had to be sanctioned by Parliament. It is clear that Victor Emanuel had no alternative but to agree to these clauses, even though he could not at first get a majority to support him in the Lower House. To secure it, he had to dissolve Parliament twice, and to make a special appeal to the electorate in his 'proclamation of Moncalieri' of November 1849, which virtually threatened that the constitution would be withdrawn if a majority willing to approve the ratification was not returned. He succeeded. In this sense too the King saved the Constitution. But he had very little freedom of manoeuvre (Docs 13A, 13B).[1]

The hastily-composed constitution was a very moderate document, resembling the French constitution of 1814. There were two Chambers. The king appointed the upper house. The ministers were stated to be simply 'responsible', that is, they were not stated to be responsible to parliament; and in fact the clause was interpreted to mean that they were responsible separately to the king. The franchise was restricted by a literacy qualification and a tax-paying qualification. The electorate amounted to about 2¼ per cent of the population, of whom about a half were likely to vote. This was a smaller proportion than under the unreformed constitution of Britain before 1832.[2]

However moderate, this was the only constitution in Italy after 1849. Its mere existence gave Piedmont a special role. She had a reasonably free press, and exiles from other Italian states could safely live in Piedmont and campaign there for reforms elsewhere. During the fifties

[1] H. M. Smyth, 'The Armistice of Novara: A Legend of a Liberal King', *Journal of Modern History*, 1935. This article is fundamental, but it gives too little weight to the negotiations after the original armistice of Novara.

[2] The constitution is partly printed in Mack Smith, *The Making of Italy*, pp. 136–9 and in Woolf, *The Italian Risorgimento*, pp. 51–3.

the universities of Piedmont, and its newspapers, came to be dominated by men from other parts of Italy. The state became much more Italian in character. Further the fact that her government was constitutional ensured her a degree of sympathy from Britain. Even Queen Victoria felt this.[3]

Massimo d'Azeglio was the Prime Minister who advised the issue of the proclamation of Moncalieri and who set the new regime on its feet. His Ministry lasted until 1852, and particularly distinguished itself by reversing the trend of Charles Albert's ecclesiastical measures. Perhaps the most important fact about it, though, was that from 1850 for nearly two years it included Cavour, whose policies dominated it and who moulded the history of Piedmont as Prime Minister from 1852 (except for a few months in 1859–60) until his death in 1861.

Camillo di Cavour[4] was born in Piedmont under Napoleonic rule in 1810. He was the younger son of an aristocratic family which had acquired a good deal of monastic land during the revolutionary period. He first took up a military career, but did not pursue it after Charles Albert had shown what his attitude was to liberal officers. He then devoted himself to farming, financial speculation, travel, and political and economic reading and writing. He spent much time in Switzerland. He became an admirer of the English economic and political system, especially when under the aegis of Peel. Although he had begun to establish himself as a public figure in the Piedmont of the forties, he did not, and could not, take an active part in politics until elections were held in 1848 under the new constitution. Once elected, he made a reputation and a following for himself in Parliament, as a non-revolutionary progressive. He seemed to have become virtually indispensable when he was given office as Minister of Marine, Commerce and Agriculture in 1850.

He was a generally cheerful and self-confident man, very energetic and with broad interests. His abilities as a writer, speaker and theorist were considerable. As a politician, diplomatist and statesman he eventually proved outstanding, perhaps a genius. He usually behaved

[3] D. Beales, *England and Italy*, p. 35.

[4] In English, as well as the volumes of A. J. Whyte already cited, there is W. R. Thayer, *The Life and Times of Cavour* (Boston, Mass., U.S.A., 1911). Both these works are full and well-grounded in the sources available when they were written, but neither could be called impartial and neither used the modern National Edition of Cavour's letters.

In Italian, there is a bibliographical article in *Nuove Questioni*, Vol. I, by R. Romeo. The most important single work is A. Omodeo, *L'opera politica del conte di Cavour* (Florence, 1940), 2 vols, which unfortunately goes no further than 1857.

as a middle-of-the-road man, a realist, a compromiser. But it was occasionally revealed, at moments of great stress, as after the truce of Villafranca in 1859, that there was a passionate and barely governable intensity behind the cool façade. At such times he lost command of himself, 'had a *coup de tête*,' threw crockery about, and appeared to lose all reasonableness and judgement. These episodes make it easier to understand his motives and sympathize with his day-to-day political deviousness.

He sometimes gave the impression that there was no principle he would not waive. However, he always insisted on working with the aid of Parliament in a constitutional state. He was by inclination and conviction a free trader, a secularist and a respecter of public opinion. But he was also a monarchist and an enemy to democracy and revolution. It was not always easy to reconcile these attitudes, especially in the Piedmontese situation. He often acted first, and only afterwards asked for an indemnity from Parliament—as over the fortifications he erected against Austria. He overruled and deceived his Cabinet. At the most critical periods he kept Parliament prorogued and used emergency powers. He often paid more attention to the King than to the Chambers, and sometimes seemed to value the latter only as a weapon to use on occasion against the King. He bribed newspapers. He suppressed Mazzini's journals one after the other. He rigged elections. He certainly did not behave according to the theoretical canons of modern British constitutionalism. He gained his first Cabinet promotion, to Minister of Finance in 1851, by working against his colleague, the previous holder of the post, from within the Cabinet. When he was out of office in 1852, he did not go into opposition; he left the country and awaited a call to return. He became Prime Minister, as will be seen, by somewhat dubious compromises with other Parliamentarians and the King. But many of his actions are readily defensible on the plea of national security, in the context of Piedmont's precarious international situation. It should be remembered also that the constitution did not make ministers responsible to Parliament.[5]

Cavour's role, and the way he played it, will become clearer as some of the more important incidents of his career are described and discussed. His ministerial promotion in 1851 illustrated not only his powers of intrigue but also his financial competence and his awareness of public opinion in other parts of Italy than Piedmont. The question concerned the raising of a loan to help pay for railway-building. The Azeglio Government was negotiating, as on earlier occasions, with the Rothschilds, for a loan to be raised chiefly in France. Cavour

[5] Mack Smith, 'Cavour and Parliament', *Cambridge Historical Journal*, 1957.

succeeded in getting a better quotation for borrowing in Britain and Italy.

How he became Prime Minister is a complex story. Again, working from within the Azeglio Ministry, he made overtures to the Centre Left under Urbano Rattazzi, who had served as a Minister during the second war with Austria and was considered an extremist. Eventually Cavour's position within the Ministry became impossible. He then resigned, went abroad, and had to be summoned back at the end of 1852 to form his own government. The basis of his power until 1857 was his alliance with Rattazzi. In order to get into power, however, he had had to compromise one of his principles, his secularism, for the sake of satisfying the King and maintaining moderate support. In 1850 Azeglio's government, with Cavour's encouragement, had passed the Siccardi laws which abolished the ecclesiastical privileges granted by Charles Albert. The final crisis of 1851 was partly provoked by a dispute between the King and Azeglio over a further step towards secularization, the introduction of civil marriage. When accepting office, Cavour agreed not to press this measure.

He has been blamed not only for this, but also for the manner of his mustering support. He himself was very proud of making his coalition or Connubio ('marriage') with Rattazzi, which set a precedent for many similar manoeuvres in Italian politics. Political scientists have dignified the method as a system called 'Trasformismo'. But it has been objected that Piedmont, and then Italy, would have been better off with something more like a two-party system. Such systems, however, are slow to develop, and could hardly be expected to appear in a country like Piedmont, where there was an extreme clerical Right and an extreme revolutionary Left, both of which despised the constitution. The only possible kinds of parliamentary government in the Piedmont of the fifties, as later in Italy, were various types of centre coalition.

Ecclesiastical policy continued to cause Cavour trouble. In 1854–5 he tried to raise money for participation in the Crimean war by suppressing 'useless' monasteries. Victor Emanuel wrote privately to the Pope, and eventually the church offered as a gift an equivalent sum to the expected proceeds of the dissolution. Cavour, outmanoeuvred, resigned. But the King failed to form a more conservative ministry, and Cavour returned to power, agreeing to limit his demands. In the election of 1857 clericals were highly successful, and Cavour maintained his majority only by finding excuses for invalidating many of the returns and by dropping Rattazzi and taking in representatives of the Right.

In economic affairs Cavour achieved much in the fifties. While a minister under Azeglio he made new commercial treaties with the main

European powers, and considerably lowered the Piedmontese tariff in the process. But he did not come near to a policy of complete Free Trade, because he required so much money for his military and other expenditure. He spent a great deal on the navy, and especially on improving the port of La Spezia as a rival to disloyal Genoa. He also assisted railway-building. By 1860 Piedmont, with 800 kilometres of track, had more than any other state of the peninsula, and a third of the tally for the whole of Italy. As well as by high taxation, Cavour financed his policies by incurring deliberate deficits. Piedmont's trade trebled in value during the fifties, and her industries flourished.[6]

No other Italian state competed in interest with Piedmont in this period, whether politically or economically. From being exceptionally obscurantist, she became the unchallenged leader of Italy, easily the most liberal and progressive state in the peninsula. It is true that the island of Sardinia remained exceedingly backward; that clericalism was still unusually powerful in Piedmont; that Savoy, Genoa and the island of Sardinia all displayed distrust of rule from Turin; that the traditional wish for aggrandizement survived; and that the constitution was a narrow document. But, all the same, no government in Italy had ever shown itself at once so reformist and so independent, even Italian, in its policy towards other powers. So, although the preservation of the constitution had in 1848–9 seemed acceptable to moderate conservatives both in Austria and in Piedmont, the logic of its continuing existence led Piedmont towards radicalism and ever greater hostility to Austria.

[6]D. Demarco, 'L'economia e la finanza degli stati italiani dal 1848 al 1860' in *Nuove Questioni*, Vol. I.

7

Cavour's Foreign Policy and Unification 1852-61

Cavour's domestic achievements were finally overshadowed by his extraordinary triumphs in foreign policy. No ministerial career has ever been more successful than his. Having become Prime Minister when his small country was struggling to recover from the defeats of 1848–9, he died leaving his King ruler of a state five times as large, able to claim rank as one of the Great Powers. It is not surprising that many historians, as well as patriotic propagandists should have represented unification as the direct outcome of Cavour's long-matured plans.

Clearly, though, it was not. In the first place, Cavour, when he came to power, had very little knowledge or experience of foreign affairs; and he seems to have had no very specific ideas about it. He hoped for the eventual attainment of Italian independence. He had no doubt that Austria was the enemy. He was conscious that in 1848–9 Piedmont had lacked an ally. He placed his hopes on France. He appreciated that Piedmont's international position made it comparatively safe for her to risk war and aim at aggrandizement, since the other powers were unlikely to allow her to lose any of her existing territory even if she was defeated. He had spoken of the possibility that Italy would benefit by 'a remodelling of Europe'.[1] But he developed definite projects only as his experience increased and the situation became more favourable. In any case, he showed his skill less in forward planning than in brilliant exploitation of changing circumstances.

His first important diplomatic problem was the question of Piedmontese involvement in the Crimean War. The war, between Britain and France on one side and Russia on the other, began early in 1854. In

[1] In his famous review of 1846 of Count Petitti's book on railways in Italy, printed in translation in Mack Smith, *Making of Italy* (quotation from p. 102).

Process of Italian Unification
At the Beginning of 1859

b. After July, 1859

After March, 1860

d. After October, 1860

January 1855 Piedmont joined in on the French side. All she did was *adhere* to the existing alliance between Britain and France; she obtained no promises or concessions from the allies. Some Piedmontese troops fought with no particular distinction in the Crimea. At the end of the war, Piedmont was represented at the Peace Congress at Paris, which was remarkable in view of her size and status. Cavour was her chief delegate, and he had the opportunity to make some complaints to the Congress about the condition of other parts of Italy. Certain historians, such as A. J. Whyte in English, have maintained that the Piedmontese intervention in the war was part of a deep-laid plan of Cavour's to intrude himself into the Congress where, it is claimed, his efforts contributed greatly to unification.

The case is in fact quite different. Early in the war, Cavour was unofficially asked whether Piedmont would send troops to help Britain and France against Russia. Personally, he wanted to. But he found that his colleagues would not agree. The reason for the request was that the allies preferred other countries to do their fighting for them so far as possible, and they thought Piedmont's troops would make as good mercenaries as any others. A second reason, which made the approach to Piedmont of special significance, was that Britain and France considered it vital to have the support of Austria against Russia. This plainly depended on effectively neutralizing Piedmont in Italy, so that Austria could safely turn her military attention eastwards. Piedmont, therefore, was being asked to engage in the war precisely in order to divert her from Italian affairs. Cavour and others in Piedmont nurtured some hope that she might thereby gain a small territorial reward. But in the short term it was difficult to regard the proposal as contributing to Italian independence. The best prospect it offered was long-term, that Piedmont, by associating herself actively with the allies, would be able to derive benefit from any liberalization of treaty arrangements that might follow an Anglo-French victory. Anyhow, this unofficial request made no progress for some months, while the allies occupied themselves with cajoling Austria. No specific bribes, except a subsidy, were offered to Piedmont.

Then, at the end of 1854, a new stage opened. The allies' need for troops had become still more pressing, as the losses in the Crimean winter mounted. But, more decisive, Austria had been induced to join the alliance, at least on paper. In order to procure this result, France had given a guarantee of Austrian possessions in Italy. It remained true that, if Austria was to be persuaded to send troops to the Russian front, Piedmont had to be neutralized. But now she was in a much weaker position. With Austria and France actually in alliance, the whole advantage of her situation as a buffer-state between them was lost. Further, it was even more difficult than before to represent adhesion to the alliance against Russia as a step likely to advance the cause of Italian independence. Piedmont, after all, was being asked to ally with the national enemy, Austria. Still, in the circumstances, the pressure was irresistible. So, at least, it seemed to Cavour, and realistically it is hard to disagree. He prevailed upon his Cabinet to join the alliance, virtually without conditions, except as to a British loan. His Foreign Secretary, Dabormida, resigned, and Cavour took the post as well as his others.

There is a domestic political dimension to the story also. As usual, the international and internal situations of Piedmont were inseparable. Victor Emanuel wanted war from the start. He was also looking for means to get rid of Cavour, as too liberal. He induced a Right-wing group to prepare themselves to displace Cavour and provide the King with his war. Cavour only remained in office by doing as the King wanted, despite objections from his Cabinet. But it should be remembered that Cavour had been in favour of the alliance from the start, though for more subtle reasons than Victor Emanuel's simple-minded desire for military glory.[2] A few months later, as has been seen, Cavour survived another threat from the King and the Right, over the law suppressing monasteries to pay for the war.

When the war ended early in 1856, too soon for Cavour's liking, before Piedmont had been able to make a mark, and with Russia still in the fight, he set off for the Congress of Paris. Piedmont was allowed to be represented only as a subordinate ally of the victors, and Cavour was not hopeful of the outcome. In open session he achieved very little. He himself spoke once of the woes of Italy, and so did the British representative, Lord Clarendon. But in so far as the cause of Italian independence derived much advantage from the Congress, it was through informal contacts. Cavour believed he had won promises of support from both Clarendon and the Emperor Napoleon III of France. There proved to be more substance in the vague words of the latter than in those of the former. But Britain and France decided to make the

[2] For a full account it is necessary to recur to Omodeo, *Opera politica di Cavour*. Most of the documents of the negotiation for the treaty are in F. Curato (ed.), *Le relazioni diplomatiche tra la Gran Bretagna ed il Regno di Sardegna dal 1852 al 1856* (Turin, 1956), Vol. II, containing Hudson's correspondence as British Minister to Sardinia, translated into Italian, and (inconveniently called almost the same thing) F. Curato (ed.), *Le relazioni diplomatiche fra la Gran Bretagna e il Regno di Sardegna*, III Series (1848–1860), Vols V (Rome, 1968) and VI (Rome, 1969), with a wider but less complete selection of diplomatic documents in the original languages. Mack Smith, *Making of Italy*, pp. 184–200.

gesture of breaking off diplomatic relations with the Kingdom of the Two Sicilies, on the ground that it was tyrannically governed. Far from having won a diplomatic triumph at Paris, Cavour was doubtful before the event whether he could present a good enough case to the Piedmontese Parliament to get approval of the peace.[3]

The Crimean War, however, did make possible the Italian war of 1859, and so unification. For it definitively upset the settlement made by the Treaties of Vienna. Russia, in 1848–9 the strongest and most single-minded defender of the *status quo*, having now been defeated and humiliated, became a revisionist power. France remained so. Austria was thus no longer on the side of the stronger in her determination to preserve her position exactly as it had been established in 1815.

More specifically, it became possible—indeed it was the logical next step for Napoleon III—for France to ally with Piedmont against Austria. It is excessively difficult in the case of Napoleon III to disentangle personal factors from others. Superficially, his character and aims were all-important. He was born in 1808, the nephew of the great Napoleon. Like Mazzini he grew up with an irrational faith in a cause. But Napoleon III's cause was that of a dynasty, or of himself, rather than that of a nation or a principle. Like Mazzini again, he engaged in plots designed to provoke popular insurrections. He was even involved in the revolution of 1831 in the Romagna, as a sort of Carbonaro. He considered support for Italian freedom to be part of the hereditary policy of his dynasty. But his chief *coups* were those of 1836 and 1840, intended to bring down King Louis Philippe and place himself on the French throne, enterprises which ended in ludicrous failure, and the *coup d'état* of 1851 which made him dictator. In 1848 he had been elected, by a large majority, the first President of the Republic created by the French revolution of that year. Like some modern dictators, he had an intuitive appreciation of possibilities which ordinary experts failed to see. He had a Foreign Secretary, but he kept from him his real intentions, and used the official foreign policy as a screen for his own. His name required him to seek a revision of the Vienna settlement. He had often spoken of doing something for Italy, and did so to Cavour on more than one occasion in the mid-fifties. But it appears to have been a chance incident that stirred him into action. In January 1858 an Italian revolutionary, Felice Orsini, made an attempt to assassinate him. Orsini conceived of the Emperor as a traitor to the Italian cause to which in his youth he had sworn support. Napoleon allowed Orsini to

[3] Mack Smith, 'Cavour and Clarendon: English Documents on the Italian Question at the Congress of Paris', *Atti del XXXV Congresso di Storia del Risorgimento Italiano* (Rome, 1957), pp. 235–49; *Making of Italy*, pp. 201–8.

be guillotined, but he also encouraged him to write an appeal to him to help Italy, which Napoleon had published. While he made a great fuss with England and Piedmont because their liberal political systems made possible the planning of such outrages as Orsini's, he also began to make more serious preparations to intervene in Italy. It was Napoleon personally who arranged a meeting with Cavour at Plombières (a French spa on the border with Switzerland) on July 21, 1858, and there the war of 1859 was planned; and he continued to pursue the policy against the advice of his ministers and in face of public disapproval. Although he exacted the cession of Savoy and Nice from Piedmont as the price of his assistance, he remained throughout 1859 and 1860, even when developments in Italy went beyond his original aims, sympathetic to the problems of Cavour and other Italian leaders.

It was not of course purely and simply a matter of Napoleon's initiatives. He did, after all, get elected with over 5,000,000 votes in 1848, and his attempt to revive some of the glories of his uncle's reign, to overturn the settlement of 1815 and resume French expansion evidently commanded much support in France. His Italian schemes chimed in with one tradition of French foreign policy. But it is difficult to believe that, if Napoleon had died at any time before May 1859, the war with Austria would have occurred at all. It was enormously fortunate for Cavour and for the cause of Italian independence that Napoleon III ruled France in the 1850s; and that he did so was itself the result of quite extraordinary luck.[4]

While Napoleon was talking with Cavour at Plombières, he received an alarmed note from his Foreign Secretary warning him that Cavour had arrived in the town. Cavour's own diplomacy was scarcely less conspiratorial. He told only the King and one other Cabinet Minister of the meeting. Three days later he sat down in a hotel in Baden and wrote an immensely long letter to Victor Emanuel, telling him what had passed. This is printed as Document 14. It throws much light on the methods of the two statesmen, and incidentally on the depths to which dynasticism had sunk.

Apart from the dynastic question, it was a plot of almost pure *Realpolitik*. There is no sign that there was any consideration given to the liberal and constitutional development of Italy. Piedmont was to expand over northern Italy once Austria had been defeated, but the Pope and the King of Naples were to be left alone, and no stipulations

[4] The role of Napoleon III is very difficult to fathom. Perhaps the best Life in English is by J. M. Thompson, *Louis Napoleon and the Second Empire* (Oxford, 1954), and the best source for his Italian attitudes the *Carteggio Cavour-Nigra dal 1858 al 1861* (Bologna, 1926–9), 4 vols.

were made about the form of government to be adopted in the proposed Kingdom of Central Italy. It is fair to Cavour to assume that he took it as axiomatic that the area under Piedmontese control would be constitutionally governed. But the same can hardly be said of the rest of the peninsula. Nor does it appear from Cavour's letter that the idea of unification was entertained. He does tell the King that the proposed arrangements will give Piedmont effective dominance in Italy. But there is no hint of more direct control. It seems certain that neither Napoleon nor Cavour expected or desired unification at this stage. Throughout, as far as his intentions can be read, Napoleon seems to have assumed that a united Italy would be a potential threat to France; and Cavour habitually spoke of unification as nonsense. If Cavour had reservations about the proposals, they concerned the idea of establishing a federation of the remaining Italian states, which he never warmly supported, and the erection of an independent central Italian kingdom.

As such schemes go, it was successful. Massa and Carrara refused to oblige with the expected insurrection, and for a time Napoleon and Cavour despaired of provoking Austria to war. She had lately liberalized the administration of her Italian territories and her position there was strong. Napoleon was positive that it would be unsafe to go to war unless Austria appeared to be the aggressor, and in the middle of April 1859 he forced Cavour to agree to disarm if Austria would do the same. The position seemed hopeless. Then Austria saved the day by sending an ultimatum demanding the unilateral disarmament of Piedmont. The war took place over a period of two months, from the very end of April to early July. The armies of France and Piedmont, assisted this time by Garibaldian irregulars, conquered Lombardy, winning two major battles at Magenta and Solferino. Under cover of the war revolts occurred in Tuscany, Modena, Parma and the Romagna. The rulers of the Duchies left their states, and Piedmontese commissioners and soldiers moved in to run the provisional governments which took their place or, in the Romagna, defied the Pope at Rome (Doc. 15). By the end of June they were all well established.

Then difficulties arose. Napoleon believed that Prussia would intervene on the side of Austria if his success continued. He also distrusted Cavour's activities in the duchies, especially in Tuscany which, according to the Plombières scheme, was not to be part of the enlarged Piedmont. He suddenly made a truce with Francis Joseph at Villafranca on July 11, without conquering Venetia, as had been planned, and leaving the future of central Italy uncertain. Austria ceded most of Lombardy to France, who ceded it to Piedmont. Victor Emanuel recognized Napoleon's problems, but Cavour, deliberately excluded from the negotiations, would not compromise this time, and resigned office in fury.[5]

For the time being, the fate of northern Italy had been decided. During the next nine months that of central Italy was in dispute. It was a period of uneasy peace. One by one the assemblies set up by the provisional governments declared for annexation to Piedmont. But Victor Emanuel and his new Ministers, under La Marmora and Rattazzi, dared not accept these offers, since Napoleon appeared to be unsympathetic. Towards the end of the year, though, the international situation improved. It no longer seemed likely that Austria would risk reopening the war, and Napoleon, in part because of British pressure, became more ready to entertain the idea of establishing a single state of northern and central Italy. In January 1860 Cavour, now much more openly identified with radical aims, came back to power and exploited the new circumstances. To please Napoleon and to make possible equal treatment of the populations which Piedmont was to annex in central Italy and those which she was to cede in Nice and Savoy, plebiscites were held, which pronounced as desired.[6] In March Tuscany, Modena and Parma, and the Romagna also, became part of a North Italian Kingdom, while Savoy and Nice became French.

In the third phase, from April to November 1860, Austria remained at peace, and so technically did all the powers. But Garibaldi's expedition of the 'Thousand' left Genoa in May for Sicily, nominally to support a revolt. It conquered first Sicily and then Naples. In September Cavour advanced along the Adriatic coast and took the rest of the Papal State except the area round Rome. Piedmontese troops then linked up with Garibaldi, who surrendered his conquests to Victor Emanuel and left for his island of Caprera. Plebiscites again ratified the annexations. The Kingdom of Italy was proclaimed in March 1861, though without Rome or Venetia.

This was an astonishing outcome. Again, it is evident that it was not planned. Rather, it was the product of the interaction and conflict of many forces. Napoleon acquiesced with reluctance in the unification process. So did Cavour, as will be shown. Mazzini, though an advocate of unification, accepted it only with serious reservations. He regretted the fact that it had been accomplished by moderate monarchists working through diplomacy and political élites rather than by radical republicans exploiting popular insurrections. Every incident of these two crowded years is profusely documented, and a close analysis of any

[5] Mack Smith, *Making of Italy*, pp. 287–91.
[6] See M. D. Vasoli, *Il plebiscito in Toscana nel 1860* (Florence, 1968).

of them reveals the complexity and confusion of motive and causation (Doc. 15).

In English it is easiest to study this in relation to Garibaldi's expedition. Mack Smith has demonstrated that Cavour was at least very doubtful whether he wished the 'Thousand' to sail for Sicily, and that it was pressure from the King and from Piedmontese public opinion that settled the matter.[7] In general, Cavour was doctrinaire in his opposition to revolutionary activities of a Mazzinian type. Further, during the course of the expedition the international problems which he faced were very difficult. He evidently did not feel confident that Garibaldi would succeed in conquering Sicily, let alone Naples as well. It is hard to blame him for hedging his bets and keeping negotiations going with the King of the Two Sicilies, with a view to saving Sicily for Piedmont even if Naples had to be abandoned. If France and Britain had so wished, they could have prevented the expedition conquering Sicily, or, as at one time seemed likely, stopped it crossing to Naples. But it looks as though Cavour doubted not only whether it was practicable, but also whether it was desirable, for Garibaldi to conquer any province. The moderate aristocratic politician had little sympathy with the radical guerrilla leader of humble origin (Doc. 16). Garibaldi, on his side, was careful not to have Sicily annexed to Piedmont, which Cavour wished to be done as soon as possible, until Naples had also been taken. The final act, Cavour's invasion of the Papal State, poses similar problems even more acutely. Cavour had some reason—but exactly how much is difficult to assess—to fear that other powers might intervene if Garibaldi's army were allowed to enter the Pope's territory. Austria and France had both uttered threats in this sense. France had a garrison in Rome. But there is no doubt that Cavour also had in mind the danger to the Piedmontese dynasty and army of the growing prestige of Garibaldi.[8]

For the purposes of this Introduction, the main question to be asked is: how far was the unification the product of the Risorgimento? It has been remarked previously that, on the face of it, the unification was an affair of war and diplomacy rather than of peaceful development towards national consciousness. The essential precondition for the events in central and southern Italy after July 1859 was that Austria had been defeated and was unwilling to resume the war. For the moment

[7] In 'Cavour's attitude to Garibaldi's expedition to Sicily', *Cambridge Historical Journal* 1949.

[8] Mack Smith, *Cavour and Garibaldi 1860*. See F. Valsecchi, 'European Diplomacy and the Thousand: The Conservative Powers' in M. Gilbert (ed.), *A Century of Conflict* (London, 1966).

Italy, which had been controlled by Austria (except for the years 1848–9) since 1815, was a power-vacuum. The Italian mice could play again. But the powers imposed certain conditions. Napoleon recognized that France would not be permitted to extend her influence more than a little. There was a tremendous international outcry over the annexation of Savoy and Nice. Any further French aggrandizement would in all probability have led to general war. It is likely that Britain could have annexed at least Sicily, if she had wished to, without provoking reprisals. But she did not want such a troublesome territory. So only Italian powers were in the running, as prescribed by France and Britain, who had the naval power in the Mediterranean to prevent any invasion of Italy of which they disapproved. There were serious discussions, however, within these limitations, about restoring the old rulers of the duchies; about establishing a separate central Italian state under Prince Napoleon, the Emperor's cousin, or some other ruler; about erecting an independent Sicily under some appropriate member of a royal family; and about finding a substitute for the Bourbon dynasty in Naples. It is questionable, on the other hand, whether a republic would have been allowed to survive in Italy. Cavour found it very worthwhile to play on the other powers' fears of revolutionary and democratic governments.[9]

It was not, however, the international situation which determined that Piedmont should unify Italy. That situation, and Italians' estimate of it, of course had a profound influence. But there were various acceptable possibilities of arrangement within Italy, as outlined in the previous paragraph. Further, there was the danger that Italians would, as in 1848–9, demand what other powers would not permit. Some essential choices were made by Italians, and of these perhaps the most significant were those of the élite of central Italy over the period between April 1859 and March 1860, which set the pattern followed later in southern Italy and contributed much to unification (Doc. 15). It is here that the Risorgimento comes into its own in the story of unification.

Patriotic historiography has always given prominence to the work of the National Society, founded to marshall support for Piedmont in other parts of Italy, with which Cavour had some dealings of an unofficial character while playing the correct diplomat for the benefit of other powers. Professor Raymond Grew has recently given definition to this relationship.[10]

Gioberti, it has already been said, gave up hope in 1851 that the

[9] Beales, *England and Italy,* Chs V and VI.
[10] R. Grew, *A Sterner Plan for Italian Unity* (London, 1963).

Papacy would lead Italy to freedom. As Cavour modernized Piedmont and identified it more closely with Italian aspirations, not only former Liberal Catholics, but also other moderates, moved towards support for the recreation of a Kingdom of North Italy, or a larger state on the same pattern. Some former sympathizers with Mazzini joined this body of opinion. An initiating group was composed of Italians who had been involved in earlier revolutionary activity, most of them exiled in Paris in the early fifties. The best-known of them was Manin, the leader of the Venetian revolution of 1848–9. Gioberti was associated with them. The most enthusiastic was Giorgio Pallavicino, a Lombard aristocrat who lived in Turin and had at one time been an inmate of the Spielberg. He was utterly convinced that it was essential for the national movement to rally round Piedmont and her monarchy, though admitting that she must modify her attitudes of the forties if they were to be worthy of support. He financed newspapers and organization in aid of the cause from his own capacious pocket. He had a good deal to do with Gioberti's change of opinion. In 1854, partly under his influence, Manin came out with a statement that, though a republican federation was the ideal solution of the Italian Question, unity under the King of Sardinia was the most likely, and an acceptable, solution. In 1855 he went a step further and repudiated those who favoured rule by a relation of Murat, an ill-defined group representing a cause which might have prospered in other circumstances (See p. 36). Manin declared that the only possible King for Italy was the King of Sardinia, and that, if Victor Emanuel was in favour of unification, then the national movement would follow him. 'If not, not.' In the following year, during the Congress of Paris, Cavour had some conversation with him, another of the private contacts then established which were to prove of importance. But Cavour saw him as unrealistic in his talk of unification.

So far these shifts of opinion were embodied only in public letters or pamphlets. It is not clear that they had a wide effect. Just as the planning of the war of 1859 is often antedated, so is the general acceptance of Piedmont's leadership. Things happened in a rush, from 1858 onwards. It is true that Manin made a final break with Mazzini in 1856. It is also true that in that year Manin and Pallavicino thought of founding a National Italian Party. But this made little progress at first. Then, having attracted the support of Garibaldi, the only Italian leader apart from the Pope who had a really large following, it was converted into the National Society, with Giuseppe La Farina as its organizer. It aimed to set up committees all over Italy to appoint the leadership of Piedmont and her monarchy. Even then few people gave their adhesion to it until after the meeting at Plombières provoked the spread of well-founded rumours that war was imminent, with France backing Piedmont.

In older books it was alleged that Cavour saw La Farina secretly over many years every morning at 6 a.m., to plot unification. This is a characteristic piece of embroidery. In reality Cavour occasionally saw La Farina, sometimes at that hour; and he from time to time asked the co-operation of the Society. It was with their aid that he sought, unsuccessfully, to raise Massa and Carrara. They helped to arrange for the recruitment and transport of volunteers from other Italian states to assist Piedmont in the war of 1859. The Society afforded a sort of link between Cavour and Garibaldi. At its peak, the Society had 4000 members, or more.

During the winter of 1858–9 the propaganda of the Society became more intense. More was said in praise of Piedmont. Reformist and liberal ideas gave way before emphasis on unity and independence. There was more than a hint of militarism and aggressive nationalism. Revolution was a dirty word. Little was said even of constitutionalism. A good deal was made of the economic advantages which might be expected to accrue from unification.

Between January 15 and March 25, 1859 perhaps 20,000 volunteers from other parts of Italy arrived in Piedmont to fight Austria. Many of them were put under Garibaldi's command, and performed well on the Alpine front. More important, people who were bound together by their association with the National Society helped to found and sustain the provisional governments of central Italy during the agonizing uncertainties of April 1859 to March 1860. The Society had technically disbanded when war broke out, but the local committees remained in being and the whole was soon revived. The Society was less important in Tuscany than in the other areas of central Italy, and it should not be supposed that it formed the only or an unbreakable bond between the patriots of the area. But it illustrates, and helps to account for, the determination and solidarity of the revolutionaries of this period. Perhaps over-obsessed by the failure of 1848–9 and its causes, parochialism, disunity and Utopianism, they placed great emphasis on preserving a solid front against the world. Though in Tuscany especially there was strong feeling for autonomy, no permanent rift occurred between its main supporters and those of annexation to Piedmont, chief among whom was Baron Ricasoli.

Apart from Ricasoli, the principal leader of the central Italian patriots was Luigi Farini, 'Dictator' of 'Emilia'. They, with the backing of countless others, including members of the National Society, were responsible for the decision that Piedmontese annexation was the best course for central Italy, and so made its adoption in southern Italy almost certain, given the opportunity. Many of those who contributed to this decision were influenced by the belief that in the international situation only Piedmont could protect them from intervention which would remove their liberty. And of course it was true that only Piedmont of Italian states could have provided an army to keep order—or prevent revolution—in the rest of the peninsula. But, whatever their precise motives, in making this decision these representatives of the Italian drive to nationhood played a crucial part in unification (Docs 15C–G).[11]

Something has already been said of the contribution made by Mazzini and other radical revolutionaries, in helping to provoke the Sicilian rising which provided the justification for Garibaldi's expedition, and in furnishing recruits for the 'Thousand'. It should be added that throughout the fifties Mazzini, and others partly sympathetic with him, planned and executed a few minor revolts, the most important of which was probably that of Genoa in 1857. Cavour detested these attempts, but they no doubt encouraged him to press forward with the nationalist policy which could alone be expected to attract patriots away from revolutionary activity. They also kept up the pressure on the rulers of other Italian states, especially Naples, and their potentiality can be measured from the impact of Orsini's plot. But in 1859–60 the greater role was that played by adherents of the National Society and persons of more moderate opinions, including disillusioned former Mazzinians.

This is not to say that all these liberals and patriots welcomed the rapid achievement of unification through the agency of Garibaldi, nor that the Mazzinians who helped the process on its way were happy at the triumph of Piedmont. But it was not only the half-blind manoeuvres of the powers which helped to bring unification about. The half-blind efforts of patriots also played a part.

Garibaldi's success in the south has explanations quite different from those for the annexation to Piedmont of central Italy. It has always been a source of wonder that a band of irregulars—even though it eventually swelled to a much larger number than a thousand, to 20,000 or 30,000—should have been able to sweep from the field the professional Neapolitan army. Garibaldi was a superb general for the sort of warfare involved, in which comparatively small forces fought

[11] On the central Italian developments, Hancock, *Ricasoli*; Grew, 'How success Spoiled the Risorgimento', *Journal of Modern History* 1962. The period between the outbreak of war in April 1859 and the annexations in the following spring has yet to be dealt with in a really convincing manner. The publication of the papers of Ricasoli and Farini etc. will make this possible soon.

minor battles in a manner reminiscent of the Middle Ages rather than of the modern world, with its massed conscript armies engaged together over long fronts. He was brilliant at sizing up the local situation, and his personality cast an extraordinary spell over his troops. He appeared to them sympathetic, magnanimous, invulnerable and invincible. He even contrived to win the final large-scale battle of the Volturno, which preserved his conquests until the Piedmontese arrived to take them over. Of course the enterprise was such that he was bound, right up to the last days, to press forward, to attack. He had little to lose. But the phenomenon of his success needs more than personality to explain it. There is no comparable story in the settled history of modern Europe.

In Sicily his achievement was largely due to a revolt of the peasants. When he reached the island in May 1860, the interior was already out of the control of the government. He at first allied himself with the revolt, abolishing in his self-proclaimed capacity as 'dictator' the milling tax, the principal specific grievance of the peasants, and promising land redistribution. Later on, however, he changed sides, and suppressed local peasant uprisings. He thus won the support of the landowners, who found him a better ally in maintaining order than the Bourbons. He exploited Sicilian resentment against Neapolitan rule, but introduced Piedmontese laws and prepared the way for annexation.[12]

Naples was in a different case. There a larger part in Garibaldi's success has to be attributed to the loss of confidence of the monarchy and the royal army after the fall of Sicily, against the background of Anglo-French hostility and Austrian desertion. As in Sicily there was very little direct support for unification. The Garibaldians were mostly from northern or from central Italy. Southerners who did not know the meaning of the word 'Italia' cheered for her as Garibaldi's mistress. But there was only cool sympathy with the new King, Francis II, who showed himself to be weak and frightened. A reaction might have restored him, though, as in 1821 and 1848–9, if the Piedmontese army and administration had not taken firm hold of the country. The essential differences between 1820 and 1848 on the one hand, and 1860 on the other, were that in the last year Sicily could act as the base for a powerful army, that therefore Sicily conquered Naples rather than vice versa, and that when the revolutionary situation was passing and disillusionment returning, Piedmont rather than Austria could send in troops.

Only in reference to Sicily is there much substance to the idea that

[12] Mack Smith, 'The peasants' Revolt of Sicily in 1860', *Studi in onore di Gino Luzzatto*, Vol. III (Milan, 1950).

unification was an 'agrarian revolution *manquée*'. Garibaldi in the end chose to put the goal of unification before that of social reform; and he had no real choice, since Piedmontese rule was the only plausible alternative to Neapolitan. The government of the new Kingdom of Italy after 1861, based on a restricted electorate, supported and to a great extent staffed by aristocrats and landowners, did not dream of carrying through expropriation in Sicily. The large estates grew even larger. Agriculture and agrarian relationships remained backward and feudal. It must be questionable, though, whether any worthwhile agrarian reform could have succeeded in the Sicily of the 1860s. Its brigands or *mafiosi* administered a private law far more effectively than the civil service, the police and the army could impose the official code. The vast majority of the inhabitants was illiterate, and the whole outlook of the people obstructed modernization and commercialization. On the other hand, it seems Panglossian to believe, with some modern economic historians like Rosario Romeo, that it was necessary to the later industrial development of Italy that southern agriculture should remain backward, since this condition enabled it to supply capital to the north and to other sectors of the economy.[13]

Outside Sicily unification, and everywhere the Risorgimento, were the work of the upper and middle classes, with slight support from below. Garibaldi himself lamented that the social origins of his volunteers were so limited. The fact that the Piedmontese constitution, with its restricted franchise, was applied to the new Kingdom without amendment prolonged the domination of Italian life by the existing elites.

Although both the National Society and Garibaldi decided in favour of annexation to Piedmont, most of those concerned regretted that she made no concessions to regionalism in the process of establishing the Kingdom of Italy. Not only the Piedmontese constitution, but the Piedmontese legal system and the Piedmontese bureaucracy were simply extended over the country as a whole. Victor Emanuel retained the title Victor Emanuel II. Other provinces were allowed to vote by plebiscite to join Piedmont, but not allowed to discuss the constitution of the new state. Cavour talked of administrative devolution, but nothing effective was done to carry out his suggestions. Piedmontese civil servants, lawyers, politicians and soldiers took a disproportionately large share of the patronage of the united Kingdom. Their incomprehension of the problems of the south helped to account for its continuing backwardness after unification, and also for the serious civil war which

[13] Cf. R. Romeo, *Risorgimento e Capitalismo* (Bari, 1959) and A. Gerschenkron in *Economic Backwardness in Historical Perspective* (New York, 1962).

broke out there in the early sixties between supporters of the new and of the old regimes. Fear of such centralization had prevented Cattaneo supporting unification.[14]

The manner of the achievement cast other shadows before. It made the parliamentary constitution of the new state weaker that the Papacy and Roman Catholics as a body had opposed unification; and Cavour made no attempt to compromise with the church, simply extending Piedmont's anti-clerical legislation into the former Papal State. Not until the Concordat between the Vatican and Fascist Italy was signed in 1929 could loyal Catholics take a full part in politics. Further, it was felt necessary, especially in order to depreciate the influence of Garibaldi, to exaggerate the role of the Piedmontese army in unification. Though such a large debt of gratitude was due to France, and a not inconsiderable one to Britain, the achievement had to be represented as one of Italian nationals. The diplomacy of Italy has often since reflected an excessive confidence in the military potential of the country.

Many forces in Italian life, then, the church and Roman Catholics as a body, the working classes, and some who favoured regional autonomy, had opposed or given no intentional assistance to unification. Most of those who had helped the process had serious reservations about it. All of them were caught in an international situation which left them limited room for manoeuvre.

It would not be right, however, to think of international influences as being unaffected by liberal and nationalist ideology. In the eighteenth century it would have been inconceivable for the powers to acquiesce in the unification of Italy. A peace Congress, no doubt following a protracted war, would have adjudged dynastic claims as the balance of power permitted. At least three of the great powers who helped to decide the fate of Italy in 1859–60 were partially committed to ideological positions such as troubled no eighteenth-century statesmen. Austria had set herself up against nationalism—though in 1860, pathetically, she spoke of giving that principle its due.[15] France and her ruler paid more than lip-service to the nationalist theories inherited from Napoleon I. Britain, though never advocating unification before the event, consistently upheld the Italians' right of self-determination. Even Prussia may have been actuated by the motive Cavour himself recommended to her, a readiness to see Piedmont and nationalism triumph in Italy as a precedent for a Prussian unification of Germany. In the eighteenth century it was scarcely possible to imagine any ruler

[14] Mack Smith, *Making of Italy*, p. 345.

[15] See Rechberg to Metternich, January–February 1860 in R. Ciampini, *Il '59 in Toscana* (Florence, 1959), p. 423n.

being totally dispossessed. In the mid-nineteenth century it became difficult to maintain a ruler against a nation. If the Risorgimento is seen as part of a European movement of reformists, liberals and nationalists, its role in unification assumes its true significance.[16]

[16] This approach deserves further development than it has so far received. Cf. the attitudes to German unification revealed in W. E. Mosse, *The European Powers and the German Question, 1848–71* (Cambridge, 1958).

8

Epilogue

Garibaldi tried in the sixties to repeat his success of 1860 against Venetia and Rome. When he was beginning a march on Rome at Aspromonte in the toe of Italy in 1862, the troops of the Kingdom he had made fired at him and wounded him. In 1867 the French stopped him at Mentana when he invaded the Papal State. With regular conditions restored by Piedmontese annexations, this kind of enterprise had no chance.

Italy gained Venetia in 1866, and Rome in 1870, as by-products of international crises not focused on the peninsula. These acquisitions owed nothing to nationalist activity in the provinces concerned, and very little to Italian arms. In 1866 Italy's participation in the brief Austro-Prussian war brought her only disastrous defeat on sea and on land. It was Napoleon III who procured her the cession of Venetia.[1] In 1870 the Italian army had to overcome only token resistance from Papal forces. The French garrison had left Rome to fight Prussia. At the Congress of Berlin in 1878 it was to be suggested that Austria might cede the Trentino to Italy. But the Russian envoy, Gorchakov, said Italy would have to lose a battle first.

In the early sixties, civil war raged in the south. However, the new government made efforts to develop Italian economic life. It began a campaign against illiteracy. It set up a commission under Manzoni to standardize the language. But the Industrial Revolution did not come until much later. And regionalism, especially the problem of the south, remains to bedevil Italian politics in the 1980s.[2]

In the early part of the period covered by this book, although Italy was being reformed and modernized, this was the work of rulers, and mostly of foreign rulers. It owed very little to Italian national feeling,

[1] J. W. Bush, *Venetia Redeemed* (N. Y., U.S.A.), 1967.
[2] Mack Smith, *Italy: A Modern History*, Sections II and III.

although it encouraged it. After the stagnant period of the Restoration there occurred an efflorescence of Italian reformism, liberalism and nationalism, which in the end imposed itself on the rulers. This was the greatest age of the Risorgimento proper, unless the years after 1943 are held to belong to it. The national movement was advancing ahead of the governments of Italy. But, for unification, the significance of the upheaval of 1848–9 was largely negative. It taught nationalists and patriots what not to do. From 1849 to 1859 the Risorgimento made little progress outside Piedmont. Then, in the two critical years of the actual unification, the international situation permitted the political development of Italy to outrun the social and cultural, allowing representatives of the national movement to play important parts. A long period of what in the case of Germany was called *Gleichschaltung*, 'political co-ordination', had to follow. 'Believe me,' said Azeglio, 'to make an Italy out of Italians one must not be in a hurry: there will be worse to come, but we shall not see the end.'[3]

[3] Marshall, *Massimo D'Azeglio*, p. 293.

DOCUMENTS

I

Linguistic and Cultural Nationalism

FROM VITTORIO ALFIERI, *Memoirs* (This autobiography was first published in 1806. The quotations are taken from E. R. Vincent's edition, London, 1961, of the first translation into English of 1810.)

(In 1766, when he was 17, Alfieri went on a visit to Milan.)

I RECOLLECT among other things that on visiting the Ambrosian Library the librarian handed me an autograph manuscript of Petrarch which I, like a true Piedmontese barbarian, returned to him with the greatest indifference. I entertained a species of hatred against this divine poet, because during the time I attended the philosophy class, his works having fallen into my hands, I had opened them here and there and had read, or rather spelt out, a few verses without comprehending them. Echoing the opinion of the French and of others equally arrogant and presumptuous I repeated after them that Petrarch was nothing more than a 'frivolous witling'.

Besides, the only reading I had provided myself with for this twelve months journey were some books of Italian travel which were mostly written in French, and I thus proceeded to the summit of linguistic barbarism, towards which I had already made so much progress. I conversed with my travelling companions wholly in French; and in all the Milanese houses to which we had introductions this was the only language spoken; so that when I wished to arrange any ideas in my poor little head they were always clothed in French. The few letters I wrote were written in French, the ridiculous little journal of my travels was likewise written in that language; and what French! I only knew the language by rote, and if I had ever been taught any rules I had quite forgotten them. I knew still less of Italian; such are the misfortunes which result from being in an amphibious bi-lingual part of the country, and from the erroneous education I had received (p. 62).

[In 1769] I might easily, during my stay at Vienna, have been introduced to the celebrated poet Metastasio. . . . But I declined . . . either from my usual bashful rusticity or from the contempt which the constant habit of reading French works had given me for Italian productions. . . . Besides, I had seen Metastasio in the gardens of Schoenbrunn, perform the customary genuflexion to Maria Theresa in such a servile and adulatory manner that I . . . could not think of binding myself either by the ties of familiarity or friendship with a poet who had sold himself to a despotism which I so cordially detested . . . (pp. 96–7).

[In 1775] I felt myself gradually animated by a passion hitherto wholly unknown to me, the love of glory.

In short, after several months constant poetical consultations; after having ransacked grammars and dictionaries; after having composed a great deal of nonsense, I stuck together five disjointed members, which I termed acts, and entitled the whole *Cleopatra, a Tragedy*. [After re-writing] . . . the so-called tragedy . . . was acted in Turin on 16 June 1775 . . . (pp. 149–50).

Thus then at twenty-seven years of age did I enlist myself in the service of the Muses and appear before the public as an author of tragedies. I shall now proceed to point out the resources I possessed to enable me to support so daring and presumptuous an undertaking. A resolute, obstinate, and ungovernable character, susceptible of the warmest affections, among which, by an odd kind of combination, predominated love with all its extremes and a hatred approaching to madness against every kind of tyranny; an imperfect and vague recollection of several French tragedies which I had seen on the stage several years before, but which I had then neither read nor studied; a total ignorance of dramatic rules and an incapability of expressing myself with elegance and precision in my own language. To these were super-added an insufferable presumption, or more properly speaking, petulance, and a degree of violence which seldom allowed me to recognize, investigate or pay heed to truth.

With similar elements it would have been easier to have formed a commonplace bad Prince than a man of letters. Nevertheless a powerful voice arose from the bottom of my heart which called to me more energetically than that of my few friends.

'You must, as it were, go back to school in order to study the elements of grammar and the rules of composition.'

At last this inner voice persuaded me and I submitted to the hard necessity of once again starting the studies of my childhood at an age when I thought and felt like a man. But the flame of glory shone in my eyes, and resolving to wipe away the shame of all the foolish things of my past I assumed sufficient courage to combat and overcome every obstacle which opposed my progress.

The performance of *Cleopatra* had not only convinced me that the subject was intrinsically bad and would never be chosen by any one except an ignorant author, but made me perceive the immense distance I had to go back before I could make a new start and race off towards my goal as well as I could. As soon however as the veil which obscured my sight was withdrawn I solemnly vowed, in my own mind, neither to spare trouble nor fatigue in order to render myself as proficient in my native tongue as any man in Italy. I assumed this resolution because I conceived if I could only write well I should not fail from lack of ideas or their proper arrangement. Having thus bound myself by an oath I resolutely plunged, with the courage of a Curtius, into the abyss of grammar with open eyes and without flinching. In proportion as I became convinced that I had failed in what I had hitherto done, the more firmly did I believe it was in my power to do better. I had in my desk a striking proof of this in my two tragedies, *Filippo* and *Polinice* which I had writtten in French prose three months before the performance of *Cleopatra*, that is to say between March and May of 1775. These I had read to some of my friends, who appeared to be much struck with them. I was led to form this opinion not so much from the praise which they bestowed on them, as from the profound attention with which they listened from the beginning to the end of the performance. Their silent agitation and the expression of their features spoke even more highly in my favour than their words. Unfortunately, however, whatever might be the merit of these two tragedies they were written in French prose, and much labour was required to transform them into Italian poetry. I had sketched them in this meagre and unpleasing language, not that I knew it nor even pretended to know it, but because during my five years' travels it was the only language I heard spoken and because I expressed myself in it better than in any other. By my ignorance of language I bore a striking resemblance to one of the best runners of Italy who, taken ill, dreams that he is running against his rivals and would certainly win the race, were it not for the state of his legs.

The difficulty of explaining or translating my sentiments either into Italian verse or even prose was such that when I re read in this language an act or scene which had appeared to delight my auditors in French, they no longer knew it to be the same and inquired the reason for the change. Such was the influence of a new dress that the same personage became insupportable and incapable of being recognized. I raged, I wept, but it was necessary to assume patience and begin my task anew. I was obliged to ransack classical Italian texts, however insipid and anti-tragical, in order to become master of the native Tuscan. In short, if the expression may be forgiven, I had daily to 'unthink' first and 'rethink' after.

The fact that I had these two tragedies by me made me lend a more patient ear to the judicious counsels which I received from every quarter, and induced me to be present, however painful it might be to my feelings, at the performance of *Cleopatra*. Every verse the actors pronounced resounded in my ears as the most severe criticism on a work that from this moment lost all interest in my eyes. Henceforward I considered it only as affording a spur to future exertions.

Just as I did not allow myself to be influenced later on by the severe criticisms (partly justifiable but on the whole ignorant and malicious) directed against my tragedies when I published the first edition at Siena in 1783, so I did not feel pride at the unmerited praises which the pit at Turin, perhaps out of compassion for my youthful temerity, seemed so well inclined to bestow on me. The first step towards the attainment of pure Tuscan had to be, and was, the total abandonment of all French reading. From that July, in order to avoid conversing in the French language, I religiously shunned every society in which it was spoken, yet I did not succeed in *Italianizing* myself (pp. 153–6).

The long-windedness and feebleness of my style made me readily perceive that I should never succeed in expressing myself happily in Italian while I continued to translate my own works from the French. I took in consequence the resolution of travelling into Tuscany with a view to accustom myself to speak, hear, think and dream Tuscan and only Tuscan for ever afterwards. I set out with this intention in the month of April 1776, hoping that a stay of six months would serve to *unfrenchify* me, I soon found, however, that this period would be insufficient to destroy a habit which had been rooted in my mind for upwards of ten years (p. 164).

1778.

Calm and tranquil, I then set happily to work like a man who has at last recognized his goal in life and has found a sure support in attaining it. I resolved never again to quit Florence while the object of my affection remained there. This determination rendered it necessary that I should execute a project which I had entertained for some time.

I had always felt the weight of those chains to be intolerable with which I was bound to my country, and especially those which obliged nobles, possessors of fiefs, to obtain permission of the king before they could leave the kingdom for however short a period. This permission which was sometimes obtained with difficulty and granted with a bad grace, was always limited. I had already requested such a permission four or five times, and although I had never been refused it, yet I could not reconcile myself to the steps which were requisite to obtain it. This law I considered unjust in its principle, since neither younger sons nor the citizens of any class employed by the State, were subjected to it. My repugnance to this species of tyranny became greater as I advanced in years. The last time I had obtained this permission it was accompanied with expressions which gave me much vexation. Besides, the number of my works had gradually increased; *Virginia* which I had written with all the freedom that the subject required; the work on tyranny which should really have been written by an author who was a citizen of a free country; the emotions of pleasure I had felt on perusing Tacitus, Machiavelli and the few other authors who like them think with energy and freedom; the realization of my real situation and of the impossibility of remaining at Turin if I inclined to publish any work inimical to the existing tyranny; the danger which I should experience by remaining subject to the laws of Sardinia wherever I might be, if I printed anything of this kind, even in foreign countries; all those reasons, conjoined to my new passion, determined me to expatriate myself and relinquish for ever a country which had given me birth, but which despotism had rendered an unfit abode for one resolved to think for himself.

Several means of executing this project presented themselves. I might have endeavoured to get my permission prolonged from year to year which perhaps would have been the wisest measure; but I could not endure a state of uncertainty; and how could I reckon on that which depended on the will of others? I might, by means of finesse and chicanery have disposed of my property by clandestine sales in order to escape from my noble prison. But these means I regarded as dishonourable, and they displeased me perhaps also because they were not absolutely final. Accustomed besides from my character to suppose things always to turn out for the worse, I firmly resolved to settle this matter once and for all rather than recur to it again and again or renounce the glory of becoming an independent author. Once determined, I exerted all my strength to attain the object I had in view, and I did well, young as I was, though at the time I acted more perhaps under the influence of my ardent feelings than of reason. Certain it is, that had I not adopted prompt measures or if I had begun to print even the most harmless writings in any other state, the thing would have become impossible and my subsistence, my glory, and my liberty would have remained subject to the will of an absolute prince who, necessarily wounded by my manner of thinking and writing and my free and scornful behaviour, would never have consented to allow me to escape from his power.

A law existed at this time in Piedmont which ran thus:

'It is enacted that no one shall print books or other writings out of our states without permission of our censors under the pain of incurring a fine of seventy crowns or corporal punishment, if circumstances render it necessary to exhibit a public example.' To this law is sub-joined another, worded in the following manner: 'Those subjects who inhabit our states shall never absent themselves without our express authority in writing.'

Hence it is plain I could not be both a subject of his majesty of Sardinia *and* an author. I chose the latter and being an enemy to all chicane and subterfuge I took the most direct road to disfranchize myself by resigning the whole of my property held in fief or free, and more than two thirds was free, to my sister Julia, who was my natural heir and who had married the Count of Cumiana. This resignation was executed in the most solemn and irrevocable manner. I only reserved to myself an annuity of 14000 livres of Piedmont, that is to say 1400 Florentine sequins which amounted to little more than one half of my original revenues. I would have been content to resign the other half to have purchased the freedom of thinking and writing and the liberty of choosing my place of residence. It is impossible to convey an adequate idea of the delays and embarrassments which I experienced before I could conclude this affair; the legal forms and the necessity of transacting the business by letter occupied much time. It was necessary besides to obtain the usual permission from the King who interfered in all the domestic concerns of his subjects. It was also requisite that my brother-in-law should receive the royal permission to accept this gift and to remit my annuity to any country where I might fix my abode. The least clear-sighted perceived that I could have no other reasons for this domination than a desire to expatriate myself. It was consequently absolutely necessary that permission should also be obtained from the government which might otherwise have opposed the payment of the annuity in a foreign country. Happily the King who certainly knew my peculiar mode of thinking of which I had afforded the most unequivocal proofs, was better pleased that I should leave his states than remain in them; he therefore immediately consented to my request: we were both well pleased, he to lose such a subject, and I to acquire my liberty (pp. 185–8).

1787.

The want of an enlightened friend for the last two years who could converse in Italian and on Italian literature had proved extremely injurious to me, especially in regard to the art of versification. It is certain that if Voltaire and Rousseau who have acquired so much renown in France had wandered during the greater part of their lives in countries where different languages were spoken and where they could find no one to converse with in their own, they would not have had the perseverance and steadiness to write from the mere love of literature or for their own satisfaction as I have done and still continue to do, though compelled to associate with barbarians. We can justly apply to the rest of Europe and even to a great part of Italy itself, this denomination respecting every thing which relates to Italian literature. If we write pure Italian and attempt to compose verses in imitation of the style of Petrarch and Dante we may well inquire, if there is one man in Italy who could understand and relish these authors. To say one in a thousand would be too many. Being, however, an enthusiastic admirer of the sublime and beautiful, which I take every opportunity to proclaim, I would rather compose in a language which may be almost termed dead and for a people nearly extinct. I would rather, I affirm, be unknown to my contemporaries than write in the deaf-mute French and English languages though their cannons and their armies have rendered these languages fashionable. I would rather write good Italian verses, even with the certainty of seeing them despised and neglected for the moment, than write in either English, French, or any tyrant jargon, though assured that my productions would be immediately read, admired, and applauded. There is a great difference to our own ears in sounding a fine toned harp even when no one is present to listen, and blowing a detestable bagpipe however much an ignorant audience might applaud the performance (pp. 254–5).

Enlightened Despotism

FROM PAOLO FRISI, *Eulogy of Empress Maria Theresa* (1783).

This work, commissioned by the Austrian Chancellor, Kaunitz, gave more credit than is justifiable to the Empress herself for the enlightened policies of her reign. But this extract summarizes well what, on a favourable view, had been achieved in Lombardy by the time of her death.

Frisi himself had been a monk, and was a scientific, architectural and political writer well known to French *philosophes* and much consulted by Austrian and Italian statesmen.

Translated from Ed. F. Venturi, *Illuministi Italiani*, Vol. III (Milan, 1958), pp. 347–57 (with some omissions).

HISTORY leaves no ground for doubt whether science and letters have done more good than harm to society. Against the ingenious paradoxes of the cynic of Geneva [Rousseau] can be set the advantages which more cultivated societies have always had in comparison with those that still remained rough and barbarous. It is sufficient to consider the differences in the Roman constitution between the time of Marius and that of Augustus, to compare the flourishing state of Florence under Lorenzo the Magnificent with the previous disturbances, the present Italian system with that of feudal government. The simple recognition of facts suffices to show that when science and letters have been rapidly advancing the general state of society and the particular condition of individuals have always been improving. If we look at the horrors and barbarities of past centuries, we cannot but feel overwhelmingly complacent that, with human knowledge so much more widely diffused at the present day, men have generally become better, more respect is paid to our rights, our streets are no longer stained with blood, and the silence of the night is no longer interrupted by the shouts of assassins and the groans of the wounded.

In our own time it has been especially clear what a direct influence good learning has in promoting the public interest. Good learning is now no longer confined to a few solitary philosophers. Now ministers commonly possess it, and the spirit of philosophy has reached even to the throne, where it has come to direct the supreme power of judgment and of moderating human laws, and of correcting countless abuses, mostly rooted in the ignorance of the darkest ages. Maria Theresa in fact found abuses both general and particular which required the application of her superior understanding, and even in popular attitudes found highly important occasions for immediate attention.

. . . The development of knowledge in our time no longer permitted belief in stories of charms, curses and witchcraft to become a pretext for shedding human blood. Thirty years ago this was no more than an idle matter of controversy in the public schools and in private conversation, whereas now there is no dispute about it. But there still survived in Lombardy, thirty years ago, that sort of tribunal, unknown in other parts of the Austrian monarchy, which had been introduced into Milan and other cities in the state during calamitous and troubled times. Thirty years ago the supreme governor of the state no longer took pride, as he once had, in serving this tribunal as a mere lictor, but the principal nobles of the country still did so. By act of the royal wisdom and authority these obscure survivals of the ancient darkness of the province of Insubria disappeared completely and for ever.

Good and virtuous citizens ought not to forget the series of admirable provisions which then emanated from the throne. A beginning was made by resuming for the supreme legislative authority the right to censor books:[1] 'as a branch of the civil police, which has such great influence in the preservation of moral standards and of pure Catholic doctrine'. Then it was forbidden for priests of the sanctuary, who . . . most particularly profess charity, humility and service, to assume the right to punish: the private prisons of the monasteries were dissolved, and those of the episcopal courts were subordinated 'to the natural and necessary inspection of the prince'. Next was suppressed a singular institution of persons peculiarly attached to the tribunal of the Inquisition; its revenues and possessions were allocated to the maintenance of orphans, and that institution was declared 'a child of sanguinary zeal, ill-conceived and contrary to the maxims of religion and wise policy'. After the loss of its censorship, its prisons, its lictors and all its property, nothing remained to it but the mere name of the tribunal, and then the name itself was abolished and forgotten.

Enlightened policy, which had suppressed the tribunals whose authority came from outside the principality, was no less concerned to reform all the others and in general to expedite judgment. And how vast and important

[1] The decree on censorship is of 30 December 1768, that on private prisons of 9 March 1769. The Institute of the *Crocesignati* was suppressed by the decree of 22 August 1771 and the final suppression of the Inquisition is of 12 May 1775. The [quotations] are from the relevant decrees.

was the aim of the reform! How numerous and how atrocious were the judicial abuses, which seemed hallowed by so many centuries and so many nations! I can still hear the shrieks, I can still see the smoking limbs, I see the blood yet running of so many unhappy men, who by violent torture had been induced to confess to crimes they had not committed, and after confessing the crimes had been carried off to still more barbarous punishments. . . . Torture has been abolished in Sweden, in Muscovy, in Prussia, in England, in Pennsylvania; and Maria Theresa, after having abolished it in her hereditary lands, proposed [January 18, 1776] to do the same in Lombardy and Flanders.

The numerous ordinances made by her in so many other cases, to mitigate punishments, to limit the death penalty to the most flagrant cases, to prevent crime rather than to punish it, to watch over and correct delinquents; the clemency she showed to some unfortunates, even to the man who had drawn his sword in her chamber—such signal illustrations of humanity and charity make us lose sight of the sovereign rigour she sometimes displayed in the preservation of good customs. . . .

In public edicts of our time the maxim has been expounded and established that[2] 'without the positive assent of the prince, in whom alone resides the supreme legislative power in all that concerns civil society, there can be no obligation on subjects to obey ecclesiastical dispositions which, going beyond the limits of pure spiritualia, affect temporal, political and economic matters; and all such which lack this assent or a formal acquiscence must be considered null and unlawful; even supposing that they are admitted . . . they are in the same position as any other concession or law which has been made or is to be made, which not only can, but also must be changed or annulled by the legislative power of the prince whenever the general good or abuses arising or the mere variety of time and circumstances require it'.

These principles, these fundamental maxims were solemnly proclaimed from that time onwards, and the principal consequences that began to arise from them were the prohibition of further acquisitions of property by the clergy; the regulation of the economy, the discipline and the numbers of monasteries . . . the limitation of wilful begging; and the approach of the time in which society would be free of many other similar absurdities. The same principles have been even more clearly defined since then. The express declaration has come from the throne that[3] 'the reform of abuses which do not concern dogmatic questions and pure spiritualities cannot derive from the Supreme Pontiff who, except in these two matters, has no true authority in the state'.

And so too, in the general freedom which the intelligent and beneficient sovereign now accords to agriculture, to the arts and to commerce, and now that it is common to talk of liberty, it should not be forgotten how

[2] Edict of 1768.

[3] Letter written by royal command by the prince of Kaunitz on 9 December 1781.

these first and fundamental principles were rendered gradually more familiar: that all exclusive privileges, all guilds and similar societies, attractive at first sight with their false spirit of order and symmetry, tend in reality to constrict the various channels of commerce into the control of a few and to preserve industries in a state of weakness; that all obstacles placed in the way of the circulation and free transport of goods, all restrictive and protective laws, are either unenforceable or useless or harmful to agriculture. . . . The guilds were dissolved; the internal circulation of goods was made free; a beginning was made of breaking the special bonds which restricted liberty in so many places where the regalian rights of the duchy had been alienated; taxes were administered under milder laws by the paternal hand of the prince.

Industries, awakened and assisted, made continual progress. Agriculture became more intense in proportion as the peasant had more control of the fruits of his labour. The orderly administration of the public revenues supplied the means to provide many other public benefits, to erect impressive workshops, to repair the country's principal roads, to open a navigable channel through the worst obstacles on the river Adda. All economic arrangements, even those which are planned best and those which tend directly to the general good, cannot completely avoid putting individuals to inconvenience. . . . The philosopher recognizes calmly the defects associated with the condition of all human affairs, and distinguishes the defects in the execution of a plan from its original intentions. He does not usually think of light as it is irregularly reflected by different bodies. He thinks of it in the sun itself, and delights in finding it in fact pure and limpid in its first appearance. He delights in the fact that it is from the throne that shine the pure rays, the best views, the most enlightened principles, those very principles which had such results in the time of Locke, Newton, Leonardo da Vinci and Michelangelo: the general maxims by which economic theory regulates the mechanism of financial administration, the laws of physics and arithmetic govern the currency, fundamental studies of hydrometry and statics supersede pragmatic error, and majestic, grand and noble architecture is combined with ease, elegance and internal convenience.

. . . Italy had been from ancient times the teacher of the other nations. She had been superior to them all in the arts and in literature during the sixteenth and seventeenth centuries, she had also been superior to them in the most useful and the most sublime sciences. But . . . in Italy Galileo had been for a long time persecuted. The nation's natural vivacity has often served to intensify the petty passions, rivalries and envies either of those who do not themselves study science or of those who do not contrive to distinguish themselves enough at it. All those who were particularly distinguished found themselves exposed to literary slander; many of them were left with only a pittance, and Borelli was consigned to beggary; some were treated still more cruelly, Francesco d'Ascoli burned alive, Pietro d'Abano burned in effigy, Machiavelli tortured, Fra Paolo assassinated, Tasso, Giannone and Galileo imprisoned. And so Italy, ever glorious for having produced these great men, either neglected or maltreated them while they were alive.

Maria Theresa, from the studies she had been able to pursue, had derived not only elegance in speaking and writing, erudition and understanding of her sovereign rights, she had also acquired a genuine respect for science, letters, fine arts, and for those who cultivate them. She had come to appreciate their importance and utility for the state, and gave them steady, uniform and beneficient protection. She had dealings with Metastasio, Maupertuis, Van Swieten, Winckelmann and many other famous men, as Zenobia was accustomed to talk to Longinus, Amalasuntha with Cassiodorus, Christina with Descartes and Grotius. From the very beginning of her reign, even amid the tumult of war, and still more in the tranquillity of peace, she spared neither wisdom, generosity nor care, so that in all her states of Germany, Italy and Flanders, the opportunities for public education and subventions to it increased, and public schools, academies and colleges were founded, multiplied and controlled. . . .

The year 1773 was doubly auspicious for letters. Then was dissolved that order of persons [the Jesuits] who, though they never got beyond literary mediocrity in their studies, had always taken the chief part in harassing those who distinguished themselves more; and the rich properties and vast habitations left empty by the suppression of this institution were entirely devoted, by royal munificence, to public education. . . . In Milan a public school for engineers and architects was established, a society for promoting agriculture and manufactures assembled, an academy of sculpture and painting opened, a museum of natural history begun, the library extended, the observatory completed and furnished with the best instruments which have since sufficed for the largest and the smallest observations. The University of Pavia was reorganized, and without regard to expense experimental physics, natural history, anatomy, chemistry and botany were enriched with every kind of rare implement. And in Milan and Pavia famous professors were established, honoured and provided for. The sciences had not been better endowed and equipped when the literary glory of Italy could equal and surpass that of other nations.

3

The First Calls for National Unity

A. 'The "Italian Republic"' (1796)

FROM 'Termometro politico della Lombardia', September 1796, reproduced in Mack Smith, *Il Risorgimento*, pp. 3–4 from *I giornali giacobini italiani*, ed. R. de Felice, Milan, 1962, pp. 259–60.

THE people of Bologna and Ferrara demand freedom. The men of Reggio have acted and proclaimed it. The Lombards are beginning to feel its effects. The successes of the army of Italy are awakening in other populations the same aspiration. Everything foretells and promises the finest epoch of Italian freedom. Meanwhile it is surprising to see that these populations, which share the same wishes and the same good fortune, have not yet fraternized together. Why are they not corresponding with each other? Why are they not uniting their wisdom and strength into one whole, so that all may work to the same end?

Does each of them wish to preserve the remains of its privileges, or at least revive their dishonourable memory? Do they wish to destroy one form of government to replace it with another equally tyrannical? Some tiresome notabilities are too active in pressing the rights of the Senates of Bologna, Reggio etc., which are the rights of the few opposed to the rights of the many. Aristocracy as a form of government is the more tyrannical as the number of tyrants composing it is greater. Witness the horrible example of Genoa, and still more of Venice. Can it then be expected that a government founded on the natural rights of Man, which has itself sacrificed so much to regain, establish and defend its freedom, and which, since it neither ought nor wishes to interfere in the affairs of other states, must and will respect their territories, should be ready and able to liberate a people from one tyrant in order to abandon it to the tyranny of those persons who ought to have demanded freedom but in fact have not done so? The French do not recognize these privileged orders, even if Most Serene and High and Mighty, whose laughable pretensions have been taken up by certain importunate deputations unworthy of the functions which they ought to be fulfilling in the sanctuary of liberty. Their mission ought to be defined by the rights of all, which are those of the people, not now by the privileges of a few, which are those of aristocrats.

The Italian Republic ought to be the aim of all the populations who wish to take advantage of the French conquests, or rather of their own efforts, which are always the most meritorious and the most effective. Who will be so stupid or arrogant as to wish prosperity to one of those monuments of barbaric feudalism, of anarchic parties, or of national hatreds, and thus divide peoples from peoples? . . . France wants and must want an Italian Republic capable of maintaining not only its own but also common interests. Will the Lombards, the Bolognese, the Italians themselves dare to oppose its establishment? So why neglect to assist the work and to hasten the longed-for day?

B. VITTORIO ALFIERI, *To Past, Present and Future Italy*

(The 'first prose' of *Il Misogallo*, first published complete in 1804, written between 1790 and 1798.
Introductory quotations and a linguistic footnote have been omitted.)

EVEN if this little book, born piece by piece and haphazardly, succeeds in being nothing more than a monstrous collection of diverse mosaics, still it does not seem to me unworthy to be dedicated to you, O Venerable Italy. So, to that august Matron who represented you for so long, the chiefest seat of all human worth and wisdom; and to Her who represents you now, so conspicuously unarmed, divided, degraded, unfree and powerless; and to Her who surely stands ready to arise—one day, whenever it may be—virtuous, magnanimous, free and One: to all these three Italies, in this my brief dedication, I intend now to speak.

The hatreds of Nations[1] for one another have always been, and can only be, the necessary product of injuries reciprocally inflicted or dreaded. They can therefore never be either unjust or mean. They are a most precious part of the legacy of our fathers. These hatreds have alone worked those true political miracles which are now so much admired in histories.

I will not waste words in tedious and useless proofs. Experience and the facts speak for themselves. Let us admit then that these mutual hatreds act as the guardians and preservers of truly distinct peoples, and especially of those which possess comparatively small territories and

[1] In speaking of Nations I mean multitudes of men differing from each other on account of climate, location, customs and language. I by no means refer to two small towns or tiny cities of the same province, which, because one wishes to belong, for example, to Genoa and the other to Piedmont, out of foolish jealousy, enable, through their petty, unproductive and impolitic efforts, their giant common oppressors to rejoice and triumph.

populations. It becomes undeniable that for you, O Italy, hatred of the French, under whatever standard or mask they present themselves, must be the single and fundamental basis of your political existence, whatever form it may take. Indeed, until an earthquake, a deluge or a devastating comet transforms your shape, and so long as your peninsula juts out into two enclosed seas, a narrow and mountainous strip of land crowned by the Alps, your natural frontiers are fixed, and, although you stand divided and subdivided into little morsels, you are for ever One. And you ought always to be of One opinion only, in hating with an implacable and mortal loathing those Barbarians from across the mountains who have perpetually brought upon you, and bring upon you still, the most frequent and the most bloody mischiefs.

Now these (far from being the Germans) have always been, and are, the French. Three times a century they are reduced by their inept, unthinking and tyrannical governments, their natural poverty and their disproportionate vices, to the anti-social necessity of going begging with weapons in their hands, turning on neighbouring peoples in order to satisfy their hunger and to heal for a time, with the blood of others, their own sordid wounds.

In this geographical and political situation such as is manifestly yours, O Italy, whoever teaches you to hate intensely your natural and perennial enemies will at the same time be contriving to teach you and recall to you the most sacred of your duties. Nevertheless, I certainly would not have set about it if my aim had been merely, in indoctrinating you with this hatred, to teach you to esteem the French while you feared them. But, to your and my great good fortune, they are so detestable in themselves from every point of view that, without any research or the least effort, just by drawing them from the life, I can fully achieve my object and yet be free of the qualms which the idea of teaching hatred of anything engenders. For this is no more than a simple matter of teaching to know. Besides that kind of respect which is usually paid to armies whose victories inspire fear, you need show no other towards these Frenchmen, who have succeeded in arousing, even in the most timid and unenlightened individuals, as well as dread of their arms, the greatest disdain for them. A monstrous and incredible conjunction: fear and contempt. Yet it is true, and all contemporary Italians feel it.

While, then, I am teaching you to abhor them, they themselves are teaching you anew to scorn them. By the happy admixture of these two effects, may you begin from this time, O Noble Italy, to take on again something of your national aspect. To that end, from today onwards, may the word MISOGALLO be accepted into your language as signifying, corresponding to and including all the worthy titles of revengeful, but just, and true, and magnanimous, and FREE ITALIAN. Then before long the time will return when the French no longer possess such overwhelming resources and manpower, and when you have shed all meanness of customs, divisions and opinions, to become great in your own right. Then, from having hated and despised the French in fear, you will proceed majestically to hate them and despise them in mockery.

4

The Neapolitan Revolution of 1799

FROM VINCENZO CUOCO, *Historical Essay on the Neapolitan Revolution of 1799.*
(This book was first published in 1801, and the translation is taken from the modern edition by F. Nicolini, Bari, 1929, of the second edition of 1806, pp. 86–93.)

THE French army entered Naples on January 22. Championnet's first task was to 'install' a provisional government which, at the same time as it was looking after the immediate needs of the nation, was to prepare the permanent Constitution of the State. Such an important task was entrusted to 25 persons. Divided into six 'comitati' they concerned themselves with administrative details and exercised what is called 'executive power'. Meeting together, they formed the *legislative assembly*. . . .

But to devise a scheme for a republican constitution is not the same thing as to found a republic. In a form of government in which the public will, or the law, has and ought to have no other support, no other guarantor, no other executive agent than the private will, liberty is only secured by creating free men. Before the edifice of liberty was raised on Neapolitan territory, there were in the old constitutions, in ingrained customs and prejudices, in the present interests of the inhabitants, a thousand obstacles which it was proper to recognize, which it was necessary to remove. Ferdinand looked askance at our nascent freedom, and from Palermo was trying every means to recover his lost Kingdom. He had powerful allies, who for us were terrible enemies, especially the English, masters of the sea and in consequence of the trade of Sicily and Apulia, without which an immense Capital like Naples could subsist only with difficulty.

From the time of the Romans onwards, the fate of southern Italy has depended in great part on that of Sicily. The Romans reduced Italy to a garden, which then rapidly changed into a desert. After the great conquests of the Romans it began to be stated for the first time that Sicily was the granary of Italy; a saying as glorious for the former as it was damaging to the latter. . . . In the Middle Ages whoever was master of Sicily embroiled Italy as he pleased. From Sicily Belisarius destroyed the Kingdom of the Goths. From Sicily the Saracens ravaged Italy for three centuries, until the Normans united it again to the Kingdom of Naples, to which it remained joined down to the time of Charles I of Anjou. And who would deny that that separation had the effect of retarding the growth of . . . civilization in the Kingdom of Naples. . . . ? The two Kingdoms were reunited under the long domination of the Austrian House of Spain. During that period of course Naples began to grow and became an immense Capital, which in order to subsist needs the grain and oil of the distant provinces on the shores of the Adriatic, whose trade cannot conveniently be carried on—and nor could the Capital be conveniently supplied—without free passage through the straits of Messina. And it should be added that the true controller of those straits is he who possesses Sicily, since he has in Messina a large and convenient harbour, while on the Calabrian side there are only small and dangerous anchorages.

The King had in the Kingdom of Naples itself a good number of supporters, who liked the old government better than the new. In what revolution were such men not to be found? There were many communities in open counter-revolution, since they had not laid down their arms, which royal proclamations had requested and induced them to take up. Others were ready to make a stand as soon as they recovered from their astonishment at such a rapid conquest, perceived the weakness of the French army, and found an intriguer for their leader and an injustice of the new government, real or apparent, as their pretext for a rising.

The number of those who were decisively on the side of the revolution, in comparison with the population as a whole, was very small; and, as soon as the matter was committed to a trial by battle, they were bound to succumb. . . .

Our revolution being a passive revolution, the only means of bringing it to a successful conclusion was by winning popular opinion. But the views of the patriots[1] and those of the people were not the same; they had different ideas, different customs and even different languages. This same admiration for foreigners which had retarded the progress of our civilization in the time of the King now, at the start of our republic, formed the greatest obstacle to the establishment of liberty. The Neapolitan nation could be regarded as divided into two people, separated by two centuries and two climatic zones. Since the educated part had been formed on foreign models, its culture was different from that which the nation as a whole needed and which could be expected to come only from the development of our own faculties. Some had become French, others English; and those who had remained Neapolitan and who composed

[1] 'Patriot'. What actually is a 'patriot'? This name should refer to a man who loves his country. In the last decade it was synonymous with 'republican'. But it is well understood that not all republicans were patriots.

the great majority were still uncultivated. So the culture of the few had not assisted the nation as a whole, which in turn almost despised a culture which was useless to it and which it did not understand.[2]

The misfortunes of peoples are often the clearest demonstrations of the most useful truths. One can never help one's country if one does not love it, and one can never love one's country if one does not love the nation. That people can never be free in which the class destined by Nature, on account of the superiority of its intelligence, to govern whether by authority or example, has sold its opinion to a foreign nation. The whole nation has then lost the means of its independence. . . .

The Neapolitan nation, far from possessing this national unity, can be regarded as divided into many different nations. Nature seems to have wished to bring together into one small compass of territory the complete range of variety: in each province the climate varies, and the soil. The impositions of the Treasury, which has always kept account of these variations in order to find reasons for new levies wherever Nature was affording new yields, and the feudal system, which in past centuries, between anarchy and barbarity, was always diverse according to the diversity of places and circumstances, caused ownership to vary in nature from place to place, and in consequence also the customs of the poeple, which always derive from ownership and the means of subsistence.

It was desirable, amid so many contradictions, to discover a common interest which could summon and re-unite everyone in the revolution. When the nation had once been reunited, all the Powers of the world would have allied against us in vain. If the condition of our nation presented great obstacles, it offered on the other hand great opportunities for the promotion of our revolution.

The population was such that, although it would never have made the revolution by itself, it was docile in receiving it at the hands of others.

[2] The basis of the manners and customs of a people is always barbarous in origin, but the multiplication of men, the passage of time, the efforts of wise men can equally soften every custom, civilize every habit. The Apulian dialect, for example, which was the first to be written down in Italy, was as suitable as the Tuscan to become cultivated and polite. If it has not become so, it is our fault, who have abandoned it to follow the Tuscan. We admire the manners of foreigners without reflecting that this admiration has inevitably prejudiced our own. They would be equal, and perhaps superior, to those of foreigners, if we had cultivated them. A nation that develops on its own acquires a civilization of the same kind in all its parts, and the culture becomes a general benefit to the nation. . . . Foreign culture imports into a nation divisions and not uniformity, and so can only be acquired by force. Which are the preponderant nations in Europe today? Those which not only do not imitate others, but despise them. And we wanted to make an independent republic, starting by despising our own nation!

N.B. To avoid all ambiguity, this note is valid, more or less, for the whole of Italy.

The decided partisans on both sides were few: the majority of the nation was indifferent. . . .

The immense population of the Capital was more stupefied than active. It was still watching with amazement a change which it had believed almost impossible. In general, it could be said that the people of the Capital were further from revolution than those in the provinces, since they were less oppressed by taxes and more pampered by a Court which feared them. Despotism is generally founded on the dregs of the people, which, having no genuine concern for good or evil, sell themselves to him who satisfies their bellies best. It is rare for a government to fall which is not lamented by the worst elements in society. But it ought to be the business of the new regime to ensure that the best elements do not also want it back. But perhaps the overwhelming fear which was conceived of this population caused too much care to be taken of it and too little of the provinces, from which alone there was anything to fear and from which in the event came the counter-revolution.

5

Piedmontese Policy and the Treaty of Vienna

(FROM J. de Maistre, *Correspondance diplomatique, 1811–1817*, Paris, 1860. De Maistre was Piedmontese Minister in Russia. His advice was not always accepted, but his views are significant as those of an exceptionally intelligent advocate both of Reaction and of Piedmontese aggrandizement.)

THE clearest interest of the House of Savoy, an interest which it shares with the whole of Italy, is unquestionably that the House of Austria should possess nothing at all in that country, subject to indemnifying it in a worthy manner in Germany. . . .

If, in the general Restoration which is to be hoped for, the House of Austria must resume its place among the Italian powers, then that of Savoy must make every effort to avoid the proposed contact with her.

The notion that Your Majesty should regain possession of Piedmont without indemnity or aggrandizement is intolerable to one of Your faithful subjects. If Austria from one side could reach the walls of Alessandria in a short march, and from the other the least skilful of French generals could mount in a quick rush from the plain of Moncenisio into the middle of the Piazza San Carlo [in Turin], the situation would be so unhappy that it would be better to treat it as impossible, regardless of what is due not only to the dignity and worth of Your Majesty, but also to the security of Italy and the general Balance of Power . . . (Vol. I, pp. 280–1).

The Revolution was first democratic, then oligarchical, then tyrannical: today it is royal, but it is still going on. The art of the prince is to control it and to stifle it gently in an embrace. To confront it directly or to insult it would be to risk reviving it and ruining oneself at the same time.

Watch the Italian spirit. It is born of the Revolution and will soon play out a great tragedy. Our timid, neutral, delaying, tentative system is fatal in the present condition of things. The King should make himself chief of the Italians; and in every employment, military and civil and even at court, he should use revolutionaries without discrimination, even to our prejudice . . . (pp. 379–80).

The Kings of Sardinia, as Dukes of Savoy, have incontestable rights over the Republic of Geneva. These rights have always been denied by force. But the force cannot extinguish or even modify rights by preventing their exercise. In this moment of general upheaval, it would not have been surprising if the policy-makers had concerned themselves at least with appraising these rights, and certainly they would have been brought forward like the others if the King of Sardinia had been heard. . . . Instead, it is Geneva which acquires a portion of Savoy, for no conceivable reason other than that of convenience. . . .

Even if the friendship of the Powers, illuminated by wise policy, gives Genoa and Liguria to His Majesty . . . still nothing will have been done for the King and for Italy, if he is injured on the other side of the Alps . . . (Vol. II, pp. 10–11).

Poor Italy! Those who love her have done what they could; but other instruments would be needed to drag her from the deplorable abyss into which she has fallen. . . . Even the acquisition of Genoa will have dangers for us. The union of nations encounters no difficulties on the map, but in reality it is a different matter; there are nations which cannot be mixed together; perhaps the Piedmontese and the Genoese fall into this class, separated as they are by an ancient and ingrained hatred. Where will the capital be, and where national unity? The imagination tries to see in Genoa a provincial town dependent on Turin, but it does not succeed; it tries also to picture Piedmont as a province of Liguria, but succeeds no better. . . (p. 21).

In the only official conversation I have had with [Nesselrode], I happened to speak of *the Italian spirit* which is active at this moment. He replied: *Yes, Monsieur; but this spirit is a great evil, for it may spoil the Italian arrangements*. . . . It is not necessary to be very acute to see that Italy is a currency which must pay for other things . . . (p.25).

I do not believe that we ought to lull ourselves into complacency about the danger of constitutions. In the absence of very skilfully taken pre-cautions, all the nations bordering France will soon have governments like hers. The hatred which she has rightly attracted by her crimes and extravagances has caused people to shut their eyes to her prerogatives. But they exist still, and her influence, especially over her immediate frontiers, will always be immense. Think . . . how she led us during the Revolution: she suppressed the *gabelle*, we suppressed it; she abolished tithe, we abolished it; she suppressed the nobility and primogeniture, we imitated her; she took the property of the Church, we took it too. Your Excellency will say to me: *We were frightened*; but *we shall be frightened again*, although in a different manner (p.46).

It was the interest of sovereigns, ill understood, which made the sixteenth-century revolution: the dogmas of the Church were denied in order to steal its goods. Today this same interest, well understood, will produce a contrary revolution. . . .

Your Excellency can take it for certain that the frightful revolution which we have just witnessed is only the prelude to another. His Majesty must guard against novelties, above all re-establishing religious education and placing it entirely in the hands of the priesthood. . . . The re-establishment of the Jesuits is therefore of the highest importance . . . (pp. 132, 135).

6

Restoration Italy

(FROM Stendhal's *Rome, Naples and Florence*, trans. R. N. Coe, London, 1959. The version used is that of 1826, which was virtually a rewriting of the original text of 1817. To Stendhal Italy is an ideal land of love and music, disfigured by its governments.)

1816.
Italy can hold no hope for literature until she shall first have won herself a constitutional government, with an Upper and a Lower House; until the time of such an event, all culture is but a sham, all literature academic pedantry. In such a boundless desert of universal commonplaceness a true genius may yet find scope; but it is the fate of an *Alfieri* to work blindly in the dark; he must despair of any guidance from a *real* public. Free men who loathe oppression will laud him to the skies, while parasites who live by tyranny will pelt his name with mud and excretion. And yet such is the degree of idleness, ignorance and hedonism among the younger generation of Italians, that fully a century must elapse before Italy shall have earned her constitution. Napoleon had set her on the right road, perhaps even without realizing whither it led. He had already revived the tradition of individual courage among the peoples of Lombardy and the Romagna. The battle of Raab, in 1809, was won by Italians . . . (pp. 11–12).

I discovered signor Cavaletti alone in his box. 'Will you do me the favour,' he began, 'not to let your mind be seduced by the manifold denunciations against the Church, the Aristocracy and the Sovereign Princes of Italy, which you hear at every hand? Instead, enquire philosophically, and consider the six focal centres of activity which control the destiny of the eighteen million inhabitants of Italy: Turin, Milan, Modena, Florence, Rome and Naples.[1] You do not need telling that these different peoples are very far from forming a homogenous nation. Bergamo detests

[1] See Gorani, *Mémoires secrets des Cours d'Italie* (c. 1796). Gorani was an ultra-liberal [1826].

Milan, which is likewise execrated by Novara and Pavia; whereas your Milanese himself, being fully preoccupied with keeping a good table and acquiring a warm *pastran* (overcoat) against the winter, hates nobody; for hatred would merely disturb the unruffled serenity of his pleasures. Florence, which in days gone by so bitterly abhorred Sienna, now is so reduced to impotence that she has no strength for loathing left; yet, allowing for these two exceptions, I search in vain to discover a third; each city detests its neighbours, and is mortally detested in return. It follows therefore that our rulers have no difficulty in the fulfilment of their aim: *divide ut imperes.*

'This unhappy people, shattered by hatred into fragments fine as dust, is governed by the several courts of Vienna, Turin, Modena, Florence, Rome and Naples.

'Modena and Turin are as clay in the hands of the Jesuits. Piedmont is the most monarchical country in Europe. The ruling oligarchy in Austria has still not progressed a step beyond the notions of a Joseph II, who for want of anything better, passes in Vienna for a great man; it constrains the priesthood to respect the laws and to abstain from intrigue; but, in all other respects, it treats us as a colony.

'Bologna, and indeed the whole of the Romagna, are a constant nightmare to the Court of Rome; so Consalvi sends a Cardinal to govern the country, with orders to make himself beloved—and he obeys! Consalvi, who wields unchallenged authority as Minister in Rome, is an ignoramus blessed with mother-wit and a sense of moderation; and he is well aware that, in Bologna, as indeed throughout the Romagna, the Italian people have preserved some traces of that ancient energy inherited from the Middle Ages. In the Romagna, when a mayor proves too consummate a scoundrel, he is assassinated; and no single witness will ever be brought to light to testify against the murderer. Such brutal behaviour in the Bolognese is abhorrent to their nearest neighbours, the citizens of Florence. The celebrated government of the Grand-Duke Leopold, successor to the appalling despotism of the Medici, has transformed the Florentines into a race of holy-minded *castrati.* All passion is extinct within their souls, save a love of handsome liveries and a taste for the prettiness of religious processions. Their Grand-Duke adores money and women, and behaves like a father to his children. At bottom, he is as indifferent towards them as they are towards him; but they need only cast a glance at what is happening in the world outside to view each other with rational affection. The Tuscan peasant is a singular creature; this race of uncultured husbandmen forms what is perhaps the most agreeable society in Europe; and I find it infinitely more attractive than the urban population.

'In Italy, the extreme outposts of civilization follow the course of the Tiber. Southward of this river, you may discover all the energy and all the happiness of a race of savages. In the Papal State, the only law in force is that of the Catholic faith, which means the *performance of ritual.* Of its quality, you may judge by its effects. Under its authority, all moral philosophy is forbidden, as favouring a *spirit of individual enquiry*.

'The Kingdom of Naples is confined to this one city, which alone among all the towns of Italy has the tone and the bustle of a true capital.

'Its government is an absurd monarchy in the style of Philip II, which yet manages to preserve a few rags and tatters of administrative discipline, a legacy from the French occupation. It is impossible to imagine any form of government of more abysmal insignificance, or with less influence to wield upon the populace . . . (pp. 121–4).

The Duke of Modena has refused to allow the stage-coach to cut across his estates, on the grounds that 'all travellers are *Jacobins*'. . . (p. 130).

Fourteen years of despotism under the aegis of a genius rudely transformed Milan, a great city hitherto renowned for nothing save over-eating, into the intellectual capital of Italy. Still today, in 1816, despite the interference of the Austrian police, Milan publishes ten times more books in a year then Florence, for all that the Duke of Florence makes a great parade of liberalism.

Even at this late hour, in the streets of Milan, you may meet with three or four hundred *enlightened* individuals, the intellectual cream of all the land of Italy, recruited by Napoleon from Domodossola to Fermo, from la Pontebba to Modena, to hold high office in his Italian Kingdom. These sometime Civil Servants—hallmarked by their greying hair and quizzical expressions—are kept in Milan, partly by their passion for the life of a capital city, partly by their fear of persecution elsewhere.[1] Politically, they are the counterparts of our own *Bonapartists*; and they maintain that, before Italy may hope to be ready for a system of bicameral government, the country has need of some twenty years of Napoleonic despotism. Towards the year 1808, it became positively 'fashionable' to *read books*. In France, by contrast, the Napoleonic dictatorship was more lethal in its effect; for the Tyrant was afraid of books, and feared to stir up old memories of the Republic . . . he lived in terror of the old enthusiasm of the *Jacobins*. But in Italy, the local brand of Jacobin had trailed limping and hobbling in the wake of Napoleon's own victories. . . . Napoleon has asserted that it was here [in Italy] that he discovered his most faithful administrators; but then, he had not stolen away their freedom, nor brought back among them a tyranny which they had abolished. It is the sons of these sometime administrators who now form the *elite* of the younger generation, which, born about 1800, is already displaying its remarkable qualities. . . .

1817.

Among the *Liberal* faction of Florence, as I understand the matter, there reigns a stout belief that the fact of noble birth conveys rights of a different

[1] All this has changed since 1820; today, a sort of *Terror* reigns in Milan, and the Duchy is treated as a colony of disaffected natives at the point of imminent revolt [1826] (pp. 145–7).

order from those of a simple plebeian; its adherents would gladly join with our own Ministers in France urging laws to protect the strong ... (p. 313).

At this point I would add from memory a few facts which I dared not commit to paper in Naples. On one occasion during this tour of Calabria, which is my present subject, chancing to spend the night upon an estate, whose bailiff was in the service of one of my travelling-companions, I caught allusions to the countless robberies committed by a gang of *banditti* known as the company *dell' Indipendenza.* The manner in which these depredations were carried out betrayed both skill and a truly *Turkish* bravado. At the time, I paid no attention to these tales; such escapades are daily occurrences in the district; I had neither time nor attention to spare from my study of the *manners* of the folk whom I was visiting. Later on, however, when I chanced to give alms to a poor beggar-woman—a soldier's widow left with child at her husband's death—I was told: '*She* has no claim on your charity, sir; she draws rations from the *banditti.*' It was on this occasion that I heard the tale which I here set down, omitting from my account many minor details of recklessness and courage.

'There exists in this region a *Company*, composed of thirty men and four women, one and all equipped with the noblest and swiftest horses in the land. The chieftain of this band is a sometime sergeant-at-arms *di Jachino* (in the service of Joachim Murat, King of Naples), who styles himself *Commandante dell' Indipendenza.* His practice is to send out warnings to the local landowners and *massari*, demanding that on such a day, such a sum be placed at the foot of such a tree—failing compliance with which demand, the house is consigned to the flames, and its inhabitants to torture and death. When the company is on the march, every farmer along the route is instructed to hold himself in readiness to serve food for so many persons at such a given hour; in each case, the tribute exacted is proportionate to the means of the victim. No Royal Progress enjoys a more meticulous commissariat.'

Some four weeks previous to the occasion on which I was given these details, a certain farmer, enraged by the imperious style of the command which he received to furnish a meal, sent word to the General commanding the Neapolitan army, and a numerous squadron of cavalry and infantry was brought up to surround the *indipendenti.* The latter, however, being apprised by a number of shots that the Neapolitan soldiery was firing wholly at random, cut their way out of the trap by means of a bold assault which left the landscape strewn with the bodies of their enemies, and allowed them to escape unharmed down to the last man. Immediately after this deliverance, they had word conveyed to the farmer, advising him to set his affairs in order. Three days later, the company took possession of the farm, and set up a solemn Tribunal; the farmer, put to the torture—as was indeed current judicial practice in Calabria before the French occupation—made full confession of his crime. The Tribunal then proceeded to deliberate *in camera*; after which, its members advanced with solemn step upon the farmer, picked him up and threw him into an enormous cauldron which was set upon the fire, and which was being used to boil milk for making cheese. As soon as the farmer was well and truly cooked, the company then obliged all the servants about the farm to make a meal of this infernal repast.

The chieftain might easily swell the ranks of his company to a thousand men or more; but he is wont to declare that he has no true talent to command above the number of thirty. He is satisfied merely to maintain a steady complement. Scarcely a day passes, but he receives new requests for employment; however, he makes it a rule to insist upon proper qualifications—*i.e., wounds received in battle, and not testimonials of good conduct*. These are his very own words (May 2, 1817).

In the spring of this current year, the peasants of Apulia were direly oppressed by famine; so the leader of the *banditti* made it his business to distribute among the starving victims a series of regular ration-vouchers, which the more prosperous citizens were obliged to honour. This ration consisted of a pound and a half of bread for a man, one pound for a woman and two pounds for a woman with child. The woman who had first aroused my curiosity had been receiving six two-pound vouchers a week for the past month.

Moreover, no one can ever discover where the *indipendenti* have their current headquarters. All the spies are on their side. In Roman times, such a brigand would have been a Marcellus.

7

Buonarroti's Activities

(EXTRACTS from the 'notebook' of one of the Grades in Buonarroti's organization, *Mondo*. Both the notebook and the organization date from the late 1820s. The police of Turin confiscated the document in 1833. From A. Saitta, *Filippo Buonarroti*, Vol. II, Rome, 1951, pp. 93, 94–5, 103–4, 107–8.)

September 1828 (On Liberty).
Man is in the widest sense free when he need take no account in his actions of any guide save his own will. Everyone desires freedom; it is an inclination we are born with, it is the surest guarantee of our happiness, it is a want that everyone seeks to satisfy. There is not a King, an Aristocrat, a great man who does not desire to be free and who does not work ceaselessly to extend the range of his power, that is, to give greater scope to his freedom. But if liberty is a general need, how is it that so many men complain that they are deprived of it? How is it that so many peoples have been seen to abandon themselves to the most violent disturbances in order to recover this precious right, demanding it stridently from their magistrates and their kings, who are as attracted by it as their subjects.

The reason, My Brothers, is that the great principle of equality was and is almost always violated; that each man is very willing to be free even at the expense of the freedom of others; that liberty without equality is a fruit of which few taste the sweetness and the great majority know only the name. There is not a Court at which people do not speak of the liberties of the Crown; not a body of Clergy which does not maintain the liberties of its Church; not a noble who does not preen himself on the liberties and privileges of his order; not a Senate which is not proud of its liberties. Unhappily those liberties are not the liberties of all, they run counter to them. The fact is that equality is unrecognized, and that there exists everywhere, even in countries that are called free, an immense class of men for whom liberty is only a fiction with the aid of which oppressors contrive for the moment to deceive and appease the weak and ignorant.

Liberty is a part of justice. Complete justice consists in equality. Social liberty cannot be conceived without equality. It seems to me that it would be folly or wickedness to compare the liberty of the Citizen to the independence of the savage living alone in the woods.

The City is for the benefit of all those who compose it, who all have the same need and the same right to be free; it is only at this price that society can be happy and peaceful: liberty restricted to some is oppression for the others; all must participate in it, equality is therefore essential. Equality in society is the equitable distribution of power and wealth.

Suppose that the Law is the will only of certain persons: they are exacting obedience from everyone else and denying them the use of their wills; social liberty does not exist. Suppose that some own all the property and that the others have only the burden of labour; the latter group will be delivered by necessity to the mercy of the former, who will command or stifle their wills; liberty vanishes. The more equality of power and wealth that exists in Society, the more influence will be wielded by individuals' wills, and the more freedom there will be; with extreme inequality goes the depth of slavery; with complete equality perfect liberty will reign. Perhaps it is not given to men to possess such a blessing in all its fullness; but it is always true that the degree of liberty which is enjoyed in Society depends on the measure of equality which institutions promote among the citizens, and that there is no liberty without equality.

Freemasonry, Carbonarism and Mondo.

Between Freemasonry, Carbonarism and Mondo there are relations which it is desirable to understand.

If one considers with care the traditions, symbols and rites of Freemasonry, one comes to believe that it originally had an object analogous to that which our order sets itself.

But this objective is so drowned in a crowd of allegories and symbols that it has been very easy to pervert it and render it unrecognizable. Moreover, the publicity of its meetings, the almost infinite number of its initiates and the casualness with which they are admitted have deprived Freemasonry of any semblance of a political stance. And, apart from certain lodges, few in number and almost unknown, in which Enlightenment has been maintained in its purity, all the others are no more than places of amusement or schools of superstition and slavery.

However, the mystery surrounding Freemasonry, the almost republican forms of its deliberations and the very obscurity of its language offer certain opportunities to those who wish to make use of them as a cover for more generous ideas and to plan in secrecy happenings as beneficial to humanity as they are dreaded by those who oppress it.

It was with this in mind that the Order adopted from the first the three symbolic grades of Freemasonry as so many steps on the way to (:).[1]

[1] (:) represents a masonic symbol - : in a semicircle.

The Order desired that every candidate for membership should be a Mason, and that every (:) should have under his direction a masonic lodge constituted by the Grand Orient of the country in which he resided. It did more. It prescribed that the mysteries of the masonic craft should furnish an essential element in the most significant instructions of the (:) whose members then bore the title Sublimi Maestri Perfetti.

Since then, the political circumstances of Europe have almost destroyed the security which Freemasonry was formerly believed to offer, and the labours have been simplified by the introduction of the formulary, so that the masonic trappings have now been almost entirely suppressed. There has survived only the duty of the (:) to instruct initiates, under the seal of secrecy, into the mysteries and forms of the first three symbolic grades.

The practice of Freemasonry is no longer a duty for us; but we are always initiated into its mysteries, and it is left to us to use this institution either to provide ourselves with a cover or to make proselytes, or for any other end which conforms to the spirit of Mondo.

Carbonarism must be considered from a quite different point of view. This institution deserves our respect. It has many connexions with Mondo, in its origins, doctrines and political objectives.

It is necessary to go back to the last year of the eighteenth century to discover the origin of the Adelfi and the Filadelfi, whose union created our Order in 1809 or 1810.

Carbonarism dates from 1812. It spread in southern Italy, when Mondo had already extended its roots over Europe. I do not know the nature of the communications which took place between the two institutions. But the Supreme Council[?] has warned us that, though it approved the intentions of Carbonarism as established in Naples or as later distorted in France, it found in this sect neither precise and logical doctrine nor sufficiently decided objectives, and weaknesses in organization, secrecy and moral composition. The Council, convinced that free communication with the Carbonari compromised the safety and aims of our institution and damaged the cause we cherish, forbade it by its decree of August 4, 1822. But, appreciating that such communication could be useful, it authorized the Legates to permit it with certain restrictions. It did more. Perceiving advantages in the practice of Carbonarism, because of the reputation it enjoys, the Council permitted the (:) (:) to open Carbonaro lodges which they would completely control under the direction of the Supreme Council. It declared itself the legislative authority for Carbonarism organized in this way, which it still considers as a means of indirectly associating with its work the more disillusioned groups and especially those classes which are the most oppressed by civil society.

I decided to put these explanations before you, to give you a perfect understanding of the means which you may use in order to exercise in the world the influence which our laws enjoin and which your devotion to the success of our cause requires.

Thus you have at your disposal three different ways of promoting the good cause outside the (:): Freemasonry, Carbonarism and the Observation Grades. Your choice will be determined in each case by the locality, the spirit of the time and the character of the individuals concerned. There is nothing to stop you from assuming Masonic, Carbonaro and Observative forms by turns.

July 14 (1824).
The 14th of July is the feast-day of *Mondo*, and it is because it was the signal for the deliverance of the human race that the Order celebrates it memory.

Our institution belongs to the whole world, and if its feast-day and some of its symbols derive from the French Revolution it is because France uttered the first cries of Universal Liberty and the first vigorous protests against the usurpations, too long maintained, of Nobles, Priests and Kings.

Such a great example was not ignored by Europe. From the first revolutionary outbreaks spirits revived in England, Ireland, Holland, Belgium and Italy. . . .

Kings, Nobles, Popes, rich men, powerful men, all were brought down by the sovereign majesty of the People, and the golden age seemed about to return. But the courage which destroys was not accompanied by the wisdom which rebuilds, and from all the vicissitudes to which the 14th of July was the happy prelude there remains to us only a sad lesson from which it is to be desired that humanity will profit. It teaches us that political revolutions are useful to nations only in so far as they are undertaken with popular views and are directed . . . towards that point of social perfection which true justice requires, that is, the freedom and well-being of all.

General Idea of a Secret Society.
. . . Those who would like to make a secret society an institution entirely democratic in its aims and forms would necessarily exclude every kind of secrecy; and, applying to this society (at open war with the civil powers) the practice of the strictest equality, would pronounce for one Grade only and for the equal and immediate participation of all in the confidence of the association. They would see in this unity the guarantee of harmony and of general zeal.

I am of a different opinion, and I think that there ought to be several Grades, forming a succession both as to doctrines and as to authority, so that one proceeds from the simplest moral and political ideas by stages to the most complex and daring and that the right to direct all the others belongs to the Grade which is most advanced doctrinally.

These are my reasons.

1. The objective that the secret society must set itself is very remote from the *status quo* and necessarily runs counter to the opinion of the

majority of my contemporaries; it can, then, be confided only to a small number of men.

2. The propagation of the doctrines cannot be efficacious and the work cannot be successfully carried out if the persons who take part in it are few in number. So it is necessary to find a mode of association which entrusts the direction to the small number imbued with pure doctrines but guarantees them the attachment and co-operation of a numerous class of initiates. Many men wish to overturn what exists. Few elevate their thoughts to the true social order, and the greater number see only some of its elements. . . . This great number may be further differentiated. Some distinguish only one ray of the true light, others perceive two, others three etc. Each of these categories could form a Grade. From the weakest one would ascend to the strongest. The last Grade would understand all and have control over all the inferior grades.

For example: In the first Grade people would be taught to doubt everything, to listen, to think, to be compassionate. They would be required to be secret.

In the second they would be urged to study, to test their endurance, to learn how to manage weapons, to defend the weak without distinction of nation or religion, and to obey the Laws of the association.

In the third would be inculcated religious toleration, disregard of danger and death, subordination and reliability.

In the fourth the initiate would be prepared for the secret of the central body, trained to contain his curiosity and asked to reflect on the object and foundations of civil society.

Finally, in a last supervisory Grade directing all the rest, the initiate could be shown the aim of the association. His ears would be made to ring with the words: Natural religion, Universal charity, Equality between all men, social pact, the General Will the source of the Law, Freedom, the origin of legitimate authority.

He would be taught that he must fight 'Despotism, pride, greed, lust, and superstition'.

By such a method the advantage of strength would be united with that of wisdom; while under the system of a single Grade the latter would necessarily be sacrificed to the former. Let us add that unless the superior grades are absolutely unknown to the inferior, their multiplication loses all its efficacy.

As soon as there are a sufficient number of initiates it must be arranged that they gather in special assemblies organized in such a way that their security is guaranteed, their usefulness assured, and that they are agreeable and interesting. . . .

8

Mazzini's Programme

(FROM Giuseppe Mazzini, 'General Instructions for the Members of Young Italy' (1831), in *Selected Writings*, ed. N. Gangulee, London, 1945, pp. 129–31.)

YOUNG Italy is a brotherhood of Italians who believe in a law of *Progress and Duty*, and are convinced that Italy is destined to become one nation—convinced also that she possesses sufficient strength within herself to become one, and that the ill success of her former efforts is to be attributed not to the weakness, but to the misdirection of the revolutionary elements within her—that the secret of force lies in constancy and unity of effort. They join this association in the firm intent of consecrating both thought and action to the great aim of re-constituting Italy as one independent sovereign nation of free men and equals.

Young Italy is *Repùblican* and *Unitarian.*

Republican—because theoretically every nation is destined by the law of God and humanity, to form a free and equal community of brothers; and the republican is the only form of government that insures this future.

Because all true sovereignty resides essentially in the nation, the sole progressive and continuous interpreter of the supreme moral law.

Because, whatever be the form of privilege that constitutes the apex of the social edifice, its tendency is to spread among the other classes, and by undermining the equality of the citizens, to endanger the liberty of the country.

Because, when the sovereignty is recognized as existing not in the whole body, but in several distinct powers, the path to usurpation is laid open, and the struggle for supremacy between these powers is inevitable; distrust and organized hostility take the place of harmony, which is society's law of life.

Because the monarchical element being incapable of sustaining itself alone by the side of the popular element, it necessarily involves the existence of the intermediate element of an aristocracy—the source of inequality and corruption to the whole nation.

Because both history and the nature of things teach us that elective monarchy tends to generate anarchy; and hereditary monarchy tends to generate despotism.

Because, when monarchy is not—as in the middle ages—based upon the belief now extinct in right divine, it becomes too weak to be a bond of unity and authority in the state.

Because our Italian tradition is essentially republican; our great memories are republican; the whole history of our national progress is republican; whereas the introduction of monarchy amongst us was coëval with our decay, and consummated our ruin by its constant servility to the foreigner, and the antagonism to the people, as well as to the unity of the nation.

Young Italy is *Unitarian*—

Because, without unity, there is no true nation.

Because, without unity, there is no real strength; and Italy, surrounded as she is by powerful, united and jealous nations, has need of strength before all things.

Because federalism, by reducing her to the political impotence of Switzerland, would necessarily place her under the influence of one of the neighbouring nations.

Because federalism, by reviving the local rivalries now extinct, would throw Italy back upon the middle ages.

Because federalism would divide the great national arena into a number of smaller arenas; and, by thus opening a path for every paltry ambition, become a source of aristocracy.

Because federalism, by destroying the unity of the great Italian family, would strike at the root of the great mission Italy is destined to accomplish towards humanity.

Because Europe is undergoing a progressive series of transformations, which are gradually and irresistibly guiding European society to form itself into vast and united masses.

Because the entire work of international civilization in Italy will be seen, if rightly studied, as to have been tending for ages to the formation of unity.

Because all objections raised against the unitarian system do but apply, in fact, to a system of administrative centralization and despotism, which has really nothing in common with unity.

National unity, as understood by Young Italy, does not imply the despotism of any, but the association and concord of all. The life inherent in each locality is sacred. Young Italy would have the *administrative* organization designed upon a broad basis of religious respect for the liberty of each commune, but the *political* organization, destined to represent the nation in Europe, should be one and central.

Without unity of religious belief, and unity of social pact; without unity of civil, political, and penal legislation, there is no true nation.

Both initiators and initiated must never forget that the moral application of every principle is the first and most essential; that without morality there is no true citizen; that the first step towards the achievement of a holy enterprise is the purification of the soul by virtue; that, where the daily life of the individual is not in harmony with the principles he preaches, the inculcation of those principles is an infamous profanation and hypocrisy; that it is only by virtue that the members of Young Italy can win over the others to their belief; that if we do not show ourselves far superior to those who deny our principles, we are but miserable sectarians; and that Young Italy must be neither a sect nor a party, but a faith and an apostolate.

As the precursors of Italian regeneration, it is our duty to lay the first stone of its religion.

9

Gioberti's 'Philosophy'

(THE table of contents and summary from Vincenzo Gioberti's *Primato*, 1843.)

Proem

To praise Italy is not nowadays dangerous to her modesty. It is opportune. . . . The burden of the discourse is in no way injurious to foreigners. The doctrine of Italian primacy is necessary for the establishment of the philosophical sciences in the peninsula.

First Part

I. Of Italian Primacy, with Regard to Action.

. . . The root of autonomy is in creative capacity. Italy is autonomous *par excellence*; autonomy is the basis of its superiority. . . . The peninsula because of its situation is the moral centre of the civil world. . . . Religion is the principal foundation of Italian Primacy. The Catholic principle is inseparable from the national genius of Italy. Opinion of the Ghibellines and of the nominalist philosophers on this point, and its falsity. . . . The true national doctrine of Italy is that of the Guelfs and the realists. . . . The civilization of other peoples derives from Catholicism and from Italy. Italy is the creative nation. Its inventive genius and sublimity of its works. Italy is the nation that redeems other peoples, and cannot be redeemed by their work. The Popes were not the cause of Italian disunity, rather they showed themselves at every time favourable to Italian and European unity. . . . How far the conquests and the temporal dominion of the ancient Roman Empire were legitimate. . . . Italy was always the most cosmopolitan of the nations. Its Primacy is founded above all on religion, which by its nature dominates everything human.

II. Of Italian Union.

Italy has within herself all the conditions of her national and political

Risorgimento, without recurring to internal upheavals or to foreign imitations and invasions. Italian union cannot be obtained by revolutions. The principle of Italian union is the Pope, who can unify the peninsula by means of a confederation of its princes. Advantages of an Italian league. Federal government is connatural to Italy and the most natural of all governments. Evils of excessive centralization. The security and prosperity of Italy cannot be achieved otherwise than by an Italian alliance. Foreigners cannot prevent this alliance, and, far from opposing it, they ought to desire it. Excuse of the Author for entering upon discussion of affairs of state. Opinion emerges from small beginnings, but must be educated by the wisdom of the nation. Two provinces above all ought to co-operate to foster the opinion which favours Italian unity: Rome and Piedmont. Sympathy of Rome for peoples, and its impartiality between peoples and princes. Italian unity would be of great advantage to the Catholic religion and bring the utmost glory to the Holy See. Of the Piedmontese and their character. Of the House of Savoy, and eulogy thereof. Connexions and relationships of reigning families with the social progress of peoples. Of the new dynasty which rules Piedmont and the destiny which Providence has prepared for it.

III. Of Internal Reform.

Of the concord between Italian peoples and princes. Lack of this was the chief cause of the decline of Italy. Error of those who attribute this decline to the quality of the race or to religion. The ill fortune of Italians even in this respect derives from foreigners. Beginnings of Risorgimento in the past century: interrupted by the French Revolution. Now is the opportune moment to resume the path of judicious and peaceful reform. Necessity of controlling public opinion. Two ways in which this spreads: the conversation of the wise, and the Press. Of consultative monarchy and of the Council for internal affairs. The Press ought to be neither servile nor licentious. The only way to avoid both these excesses is to entrust control to a council of censorship. Of the importance of the Press for civilization. Advantages of undivided power for the work of reforming States. The Italian Princes are exhorted to found the Italian union. Of the defects of the internal reforms made or attempted in Italy during the last century. Progressive decline of the national genius of the peninsula. Differences between this genius and that of the French. Critique of Gallicanism. Of Bénigne Bossuet: reverent criticism of the mind and works of this great theologian. The primitive priesthood had two Powers, the one religious, the other political. Social formula: *The hierocracy creates all civil powers.* The priesthood is the political Prime. Christ accomplished the renewal of the primitive priesthood. Necessity of civil power in the Christian priesthood. Eulogy of the Jesuits of Paraguay. The civil power of the Church does not take away the distinction that separates the secular state and the priesthood. Two forms taken by the civil power of the priesthood, that is, dictatorship and arbitration, corresponding to the political fortunes of secular states. Legitimacy of the dictatorship exercized by the Pope in the Middle Ages. The dictatorial period finishes when the political consciousness of nations is mature. Dante inaugurated the period of secular civilization of Italy and Europe. Of arbitration, inseparable from the priesthood. The Pope is the sole basis of union, peace and common laws for European Christianity. Modern Europe is in a permanent state of anarchy and war. Papal dictatorship would not come amiss in such a period; its present and future application. The Pope is the basis of Italian union. The civil power of the priesthood is not incompatible with the spirituality and sanctity of its character and its ministry. Of Jansenism. . . .

IV. Of Civil Duties.
Of the duties of the various classes of citizens, in respect of Italian union. Evils that arise from exaggerated doctrines of liberty. Exhortation to Italian exiles. Of the duty of Italians to love and respect the authorities. How pestiferous are the flatterers of princes. Of nobles. Aristocracy is difficult to do without in civil societies. Two sorts of aristocracy: feudal and civil. The first is irrational, contemptible and baneful. The second can be praiseworthy and useful, if certain conditions are satisfied. Bad nobles are the ruin of monarchies. Of the secular clergy. In what way they can participate in political matters. Eulogy of the Italian clergy. . . . Of monks. Apologia of monasticism. . . . How monks can exert a salutary influence on politics and co-operate in secular progress . . . The study of science and letters in general, and especially of philosophy, politics and history is appropriate to their ministry. Abstract study is monastic *par excellence*. . . . Of Christian tolerance. Why violated in certain countries in times past. Such violations cannot be imputed to the Catholic Church. . . .

V. Conclusion of the First Part.
It is demonstrated that the Risorgimento of Italy cannot take place unless honour is again given to distinguished minds and the direction of affairs removed from the herd of mediocrities.

Second Part

Of Italian Primacy, With Regard to Thought.
Primacy of Action argues Primacy of Thought. Only superiority in thought can be completely restored. The scientific and literary pre-eminence of Italy is not absolute.

I. Italy is First in the Universal Hierarchy of the Theoretical Science of Primes.
Two grounds of such pre-eminence, the one objective, the other subjective. The former consists in the two supreme principles of creation and

redemption, corresponding to two cycles of the ideal form. A fact interposed between the one and the other, namely, the corruption of the created. ... Intellectual and actual universality of Catholicism, when properly understood. ... The perfect encyclopaedia is not possible outside the Catholic faith. Catholicism is the unique and universal system. It is the only truly dogmatic system. ... The hieratic Prime leads us to Italy and the Italians as geographical and ethnical Prime. History proves by evidence this privilege of the Peninsula and its inhabitants. ... Of the subjective ground of Italian scientific Primacy. Of the Greek genius, which is particularly striking in Italy. Its excellence and vastness. It is the most perfect type of Caucasian, and indeed of universal human, genius. The German race, although most noble, does not possess that moral and physiological superiority which some attribute to it.

II. *Italy is First in Philosophical Sciences.*

III. *Italy is First in Religious Sciences.*

IV. *Italy is First in Mathematical and Physical Sciences.*

V. *Italy is First in Political Sciences.*

VI. *Italy is First in Erudition and History.*

VII. *Italy is First in Arts and Letters.*

VIII. *Italy is First in Speech, and its Language is the First of the Dialects Derived from Latin Through the Agency of Christianity.*

... Tuscan is the most excellent dialect among those which emerged from Latin. Merits and demerits of French and Latin. Superiority of Italian over both.

IX. *Objections Against Italian Primacy, and Replies.*

First objection: the actual primacy of France. This primacy is entirely negative in its effects. ... France is not inventive, not even in the ranks of error. ... Second objection: primacy of Germany in science. ... Cannot be Prime, because lacking the science of true principles. ...

X. *Teleology of European Nations.*

... Teleology of England: its command of the sea; its task of civilizing and Christianizing the southern hemisphere. The security of England rests on Catholicism. ...

The Ancien Regime Loses its Nerve

(A letter from the Duke of Lucca to King Charles Albert, c. October 4, 1847, from J. Myers, *Baron Ward and the Dukes of Parma*, London, 1938, pp. 65–6.)

MY brother and Cousin,

My affection towards Your August person, and the proof of friendship that Your Majesty has so often given me, render it my duty to announce to Your Majesty my solemn abdication of the Duchy of Lucca, made with the support of my beloved son the Hereditary Prince, in favour of His Imperial and Royal Highness the Grand Duke of Tuscany for the greater part, and of His Imperial and Royal Highness the Archduke of Modena for the remainder, in accordance with the terms of the Treaty of Vienna of 1815.

This same affection that I feel for Your August Person compels me to inform you of the motive inspiring me, which, out of natural regard for a Sovereign, I have had to exclude from the Treaty made with the Grand Duke and from the Act of Abdication, copies of which I sent to Your Majesty.

The freedom of the Press and the revolutionary intrigues in Tuscany, both individual and general, directed against my little state, have disturbed its peace; my forces alone did not suffice to maintain it. The impossibility of separating it from that State with which its lot was bound up; the Customs Convention recently made, which amalgamated the connections and interests of the two States; the same tendency on the part of the Liberals of the country and the Nobility who, remembering the ancient Republic, placed themselves at the head of the movement for systematic union with Tuscany; the railways which supported the demands of the Lucchese revolutionaries by bringing in less than an hour thousands of persons from Pisa and Leghorn: all this rendered it impossible for the Government to prevent disorder—or, more correctly, made it impossible for me, since there was no one in the Government whom I could trust.

After 4,000 persons, with the President of the Council at their head, had extorted from me by violence a Decree granting a National Guard and the liberation of several agitators—brothers, as they were called—I retired to Massa, whence, urged by a Deputation and with the sole object of preventing bloodshed, I allowed myself to be persuaded to return to Lucca, thus making an immense sacrifice of my opinions in the face of Europe. Received with applause that was the outcome of victory, and of satisfaction at having reduced me to the position of a rubber stamp, I was compelled to witness what were, to me, the most repugnant scenes; and, moreover, to be proclaimed with titles that were opposed to my way of thinking. It is enough that Your Majesty knows my sentiments. As the demands became increasingly higher after my return, and as it no longer conformed with my dignity and principles to continue to reside in the country, I retired a second time and for good. Convinced that I could confer no further benefit, nor ward off the evil, and faithful to my principles, there was no other path but this which I have chosen.

My abdication, however, involving a change in the distribution of territory, conforms with the bases of the Treaty of Florence of November 28, 1844, and therefore anticipates the exchange of territory stipulated therein.

As a result, that portion of the Lunigiana whose capital is Pontremoli comes to me in full sovereignty, and to it were added certain Modenese territories. I call Your Majesty's attention to this as I have accepted it in order not to leave a kind of revolutionary nest in the middle of the Apennines, on the borders of the states of Your Majesty, of the Duchess of Parma, and of the Duke of Modena. This would inevitably have been the case, if, through my not accepting it, it had remained under the Tuscan Government which, for the time being at least, is being dragged along a path which is not tranquillizing for its neighbours and which may prove fatal.

11

The 'Forty-Eight' in Rome

(EXTRACTS from the despatches of the Belgian envoy in Rome, Count de Liedekerke de Beaufort, trans. from ed. A. M. Ghisalberti, *Rapporti delle Cose di Roma, 1848–1849*, Rome, 1949.)

Rome, January 25, 1848.
. . . And, once the constitution has been promulgated in Naples, what is going to happen in Piedmont, in Tuscany, even in Rome, where the executive power is already today no more than nominal? It's only too easy to foresee. This is not all. In the present state of warlike exaltation, a condition shared even by some reasonable persons, who can be sure that, with this passionate temerity that listens to the counsels neither of reason nor of prudence, a challenge will not be offered to Austria? Then we shall have war, and a war of principles, as terrible in its effects as those produced by religious fanaticism.

Rome, January 29, 1848.
When Monseigneur Capaccini . . . returned . . . to take up the important post of Deputy Secretary of State, his first thought, in order to re-establish order in the administration and to give it greater unity, had been to institute a full ministry, on the model of those which exist in the other states of Europe. . . .

But . . . he encountered great opposition, especially among the officials who were accustomed to the very lucrative regime of abuses and could not appear favourable to an innovation whose principal aim was, if not to eradicate them altogether, at least to diminish their number.

Monseigneur Capaccini also met resistance from the top, because it had been craftily insinuated to the late Pope that this was a question of establishing a *liberal* institution, and the Pope could not hear that word pronounced without shuddering violently. So Monseigneur Capaccini had . . . to confine himself to . . . securing that the Secretaryship of State, which had hitherto formed on its own almost the entire

Government and which was unable to bear the load, should be divided into two ministries.

What our illustrious prelate could not achieve the present Pope has just realized . . . by his *motu proprio* of December 29 last. . . .

Rome, February 12, 1848.
I have the honour of addressing this despatch to you when I am labouring under the painful impression which is always produced on honest men and persons with some foresight by the spectacle of disorder and anarchy —a spectacle the more afflicting because it has had, or at least must soon have, the inevitable result of taking away from the supreme authority the little power which it still exercised.

This power will pass completely, if the matter is not settled already, into the hands of the clubs, and indeed I think one can say, without being accused of exaggeration, that since Tuesday last (the 8th of this month) the government has in fact been carried on entirely by them. Sometimes they occupy the squares, sometimes they are divided into numerous groups at various points along the *Corso*. . . .

Those who have read some of the history of the years which saw the first serious symptoms of the French Revolution are bound to find a sad analogy between the scenes which preceded the calling of the States-General and those of which we are here, almost daily, captive witnesses.

The august head of the State—and not to recognize this would be to flout the truth—is moved by the purest intentions; one thought only animates all his actions, . . . that of making his subjects happy, and assuring their independence and the growth of their prosperity. But unhappily he is too inclined to judge others by his own feelings. Experience of men and of their evil tendencies, and skill in the difficult art of guiding the great interests of society, he entirely lacks. He would have made an admirable apostle . . . but as a temporal sovereign, and while so many discreditable feelings were building up around him, I fear that he did not appreciate soon enough that, by associating himself so often with manifestations of the dangerous and turbulent favour of the multitude, he was putting himself entirely at their mercy. . . .

Here now . . . an account of what has taken place recently in this Capital.

The agitators first spread among the people, on whom they then played with their customary skill, the idea, which was soon by their efforts transformed into serious apprehension, that the Austrians were increasing their military forces in Lombardy only in order to attack those Italian states which were busy reforming their political institutions. The Circolo romano, in its self-appointed role of legitimate organ of the popular will, presented an address to the Consulta of State, asking that, in the interests of the State's security, the army should be reorganized, 25,000 men should be alerted, some of them to garrison the frontiers, and the reserve, that is to say the lower classes, should be armed. In a word, these gentlemen, who today hold in their hands the destiny of the country, wanted and still want just to transform it into a vast camp, without troubling themselves much about how to meet the extraordinary cost of such a transformation—or rather they are already thinking of confiscating a part of the property of the clergy to pay for it.

The Consulta . . . approved. . . .

[The Council of Ministers] . . . did not think . . . it ought to accept it, arguing that there was no proof of the need for such measures.

. . . as soon as the public heard of this decision . . . scenes of disorder began, and a large number of national guardsmen . . . raised, for the first time, the cry *Down with the Ministry! Down with the traitors!*

This . . . was not the only cry. Another was *Death to the Cardinals*! and *Death to the priests*! in general. . . . There is no doubt that blood would have been spilled on that day if the Pope, lacking any means of resisting the violence . . . had not yielded, and caused it to be announced . . . to the seething multitude which filled the whole vast Piazza del Popolo that active measures would be taken for the defence of the country and that a part of the ecclesiastical Ministry would be replaced by laymen. . . .

. . . threats of death were now succeeded by shouts, repeated a thousand times, of *Long live Pius the Ninth! Long live our Liberal Pope!* . . .

Despite the latest, too generous, concessions by the authorities, I very much fear that all is not over. The party of movement, now master of the field, will not check itself in the middle of such favourable progress, and its last word, unless I am much mistaken, is *a constitution*, preceded by the establishment of an *entirely lay* ministry.

Rome, March 18, 1848.

In the presence of events of such exceptional and deplorable gravity as Paris has recently seen, . . . the spectacle of a Sovereign Pontiff . . . according representative institutions to his peoples . . . may perhaps pass unnoticed. . . .

It was on Wednesday last, the 15th of this month, that the Roman constitution, signed by His Holiness the previous evening, . . . was made known to the public. . . .

In the evening the town was illuminated magnificently; orchestras established at different points filled the air with joyful sounds; excited groups roamed the principal streets singing the Pope's hymn in chorus; everything breathed an air of satisfaction and happiness.

. . . nothing would have tarnished the fame of these great and memorable days if the cries of *Long live Pius the Ninth* had not been mixed with frequent cries of *death to the Germans! death to the Austrians! death to the Jesuits!*

Regrettably, there were also to be seen, among the flags carried in the streets by representatives of the people, two bordered with black crepe, on one of which was written *Upper Italy* and on the other *Parma.*

Almost everyone, moreover, national guardsmen, soldiers, citizens, and even a good many ecclesiastics, were wearing the Italian tricolour cockade, and are still doing so; though this same symbol, two years ago, was considered seditious and, for those who allowed themselves to use it, led to punishment of exile or imprisonment. . . .

Rome, April 18, 1848.

. . . Already . . . the power exercised here by the supreme authority . . . is purely nominal. We live virtually under a regime of popular meetings, that is, in a state bordering on anarchy; and, if it was necessary for me to show proof of this, I should have a wide choice of instances. For the moment I will limit myself first to the expulsion of the Jesuits. . . .

. . . I have already had the honour of bringing to notice . . . the brief addressed by the Sovereign Pontiff to the Romans, and to his subjects in general, urging them . . . to respect ministers of religion whether regular or secular . . . . Well, twelve days had scarcely gone by after the publication of the brief when the said religious, their vestments removed, had hastily to abandon the numerous establishments which they occupied in Rome . . . ; the clubs had wished it, so had the National Guard, and the Pope, in order to prevent disorder, perhaps even crimes—since there was talk of going so far as to set fire to the houses inhabited by the members of this Congregation—had to resign himself to it. . . .

There no longer exists, except (I believe) at Verona, where these religious are still protected by Austrian cannons, any Congregation of the Order of St Ignatius in Italy. . . .

As for the property belonging to these religious . . ., it has been provisionally sequestered. . . .

Rome, May 12, 1848.

Tomorrow it will be fifteen days since the Sovereign Pontiff . . . pronounced . . . the allocution which I have already put before Your Excellency.

After the publication of this important document, . . . the Ministry, which it appears had not been in the secret of a decision which made its responsibility illusory, resigned as a body. . . .

On the same evening as the Ministry finally resigned, . . . the central committee met again at the Circolo dei Negozianti and, after several motions had been made more or less relating to the extreme difficulty of the situation, they got round to proposing the immediate establishment of A PROVISIONAL GOVERNMENT for temporal affairs, on the ground that the head of State obstinately refused to declare war on Austria and to dismiss ecclesiastics from his Ministry; for these were the two points in dispute, on which the Pope had formally declared he would not yield. . . .

. . . it is very likely that this motion . . . would have been carried, if Count Terenzio Mamiani (who, on account of his talents and of the sacrifices he has made in the cause of progress and Italian independence, exerts a great influence on the party of movement) had not eloquently urged the Assembly that such a grave decision could not be taken in such haste . . . at two o'clock in the morning. . . .

Count Mamiani had guessed right. Sleep calmed and refreshed people's minds, the idea of recurring to extreme courses was for the moment, if not abandoned, at least adjourned; the word compromise was spoken, and favourably received by the majority. . . . The Pope gave *carte blanche* to Count Mamiani to form a Ministry, with the restriction that the head of the new administration should be, like that of the old one, a Cardinal. . . . Now, since this was exactly what the Committee did not want, . . . they eluded the difficulty by not giving him a portfolio and by nominating a lay Minister of Foreign Affairs. . . .

As to the first steps of the present Ministry, it is very difficult to square them with the Allocution, since the first things they have done are to raise 6,000 soldiers and to give the Austrian Ambassador his passports. . . .

Rome, July 24, 1848.

Just as the truth, despite every effort to conceal it, always finally triumphs over all obstacles and becomes plain to all, so the present Pontifical Ministry, which rested on a mere fiction, or rather a fraud, could not long survive. . . .

The words *Italian independence*, *Italian nationality*, are on everyone's lips here. They are spoken with every intonation, but when it comes to it no one is willing to make any sacrifice to achieve either. Now, however able one might suppose a Ministry to be, and however energetic its administrative activity, can it form an army without men and money? This, however, is the *tour de force* which people wanted to compel them to, since enrolment has so far had no significant success, and since everyone declares he will submit to no extraordinary taxation. . . .

Rome, September 19, 1848.

The *Journal des Débats*, in an article which appeared at the beginning of this month, contained some very just reflections on the moral situation of Italy, and in general on the tendencies of the country, which I think I ought to reproduce here. . . .

'It is not from outside that we fear we shall see obstacles put in the way of the re-establishment of peace and the foundation of Italian Independence. Alas! it has to be said that it is Italy herself which, now as always, today as for four centuries, manages to produce her own most cruel enemies and to raise almost insurmountable obstacles to the accomplishment of the long and painful process of her emancipation. These obstacles are the absence of any unitary bond; the antagonism which continues to exist not only between provinces, but even between towns; the lack of patriotic discipline; the impossibility of achieving united action; the discord which . . . always calls in the foreigner to re-establish the appearance of peace and order. These enemies are the political parties and enthusiasts, victims of impossible dreams and mad hallucinations, who willingly sacrifice the interest of their country to their hatreds or their fantasies, like the men whom we have seen recently . . . abandoning the Piedmontese army when it alone was facing the common enemy on the Mincio. . . .'

. . . It would be easy for me to confirm this with examples taken from the conduct of two of the great parties which at this moment divide the country . . . the republican party and the retrograde, or stationary, party.

The first, seeing the failure of all its efforts at the different points where it had sought to carry its ideas into practice, and believing the ground best prepared at Naples, mounted the coup of May 15 . . . . What were the consequences? That his Sicilian Majesty, who required only a pretext to enable him to recall the force of 15 or 20,000 men which he had sent against his will to fight in the plains of Venetia, quickly seized on the coup and summoned them back, declaring that . . . , threatened . . . by internal enemies, he could not help other Italian Powers in their struggle against the foreign oppressor. . . .

As for the retrogrades, they deserve scarcely more indulgence, for they also have gravely compromised by their intrigues the highest interests of Order. . . . Their most active centres are Rome and Turin. . . . It is they who skilfully put doubt and uncertainty into an august conscience, and in a manner dictated the publication which, at the moment when they least expected it, gave such powerful aid to the Austrians. It is they also who, using the scattered members of a certain Congregation, have neglected nothing to neutralize the efforts which the Piedmontese Ministry has been making to prosecute the war vigorously.

They have not been unconnected with the anarchy which reigned at the military councils in the field and which finally brought disaster. . . .

This same party also is said, and I think justly, to have brought into play at Turin narrow local considerations against fusion with Lombardy, pointing out that the result would be to take away from that city the advantage it had hitherto enjoyed, of being the seat of the Government, substituting Milan. . . .

The formation of the Rossi Ministry has become in the last two days officially known, and it has been composed as I had the honour to tell your Excellency in my last report, by admitting only people too docile to oppose serious resistance to its head. . . .

Rome, October 4, 1848.

The bitterest and also the most skilful adversary of the Jesuits, the famous abbé Vincenzo Gioberti, not content with the complete victory he has won over that Congregation in getting it expelled from every State in Italy, even from Rome, has sought to enlarge his role and to raise himself to the level of a statesman, opening new destinies to the Peninsula.

Another Italian, the lawyer Mazzini, equally able and more energetic than the abbé Gioberti, has set himself up with the same intention . . .

and put himself at the head of the unitary republican party, while Gioberti . . . has declared himself the head of the party of constitutional monarchy. . . .

Rome, November 16, 1848.
. . . Blood has been shed, and that blood was Count Rossi's . . . who died yesterday about one o'clock from the well-aimed blow . . . of an assassin. . . .

The assassin, protected by his companions and the indifference of the people, was able quietly to escape!!

Order had only one energetic and highly intelligent representative . . . left at Rome. This representative was Monsieur Rossi, and that is exactly why he was killed. . . .

Rome, November 25, 1848.
I have just learned . . . that the Pope left the Quirinal Palace during the night. . . . It is to be presumed that he went to Civitavecchia, the port nearest his residence. . . .

[Count de Liedekerke soon joined the Pope at Gaeta, and his knowledge of events in Rome became slight.]

12

The 'Forty-Eight' in Naples

(FROM *Ricordanze della mia vita* by L. Settembrini, which first appeared in 1879. The translation has been made from M. Themelly's edition of 1961, pp. 184–8, 193, 195–8, 200–4, 207–11.

Settembrini, 1813–76, a university teacher, was involved in republican plotting in the 'thirties and imprisoned for three years. In the 'forties he became a more moderate nationalist under the influence of Gioberti, Azeglio etc.)

[1847] To show the general satisfaction at this event [a change of ministry], and to push the King to greater things, such as joining the Italian customs league that was being formed between Rome, Tuscany and Piedmont, it was decided to mount a public demonstration; and, to hearten the timid, this took place at night. On the evening of November 24 [actually the 22nd], when a lot of people were present in the piazza in front of the royal palace listening to the music, some hand-clapping started, and the cry went up: 'Long live Italy, long live Pius IX, long live the customs league, long live the King.' The shouts continued and grew louder when the music stopped. About three hundred persons walked down the via Toledo calling on everyone to follow them. When they had reached the palace of the Nuncio, they intensified their shouts. Then they dispersed quietly. . . . A great fact emerged: the police were worried, the King angrily blamed the ministry of Del Carretto, forbade the playing of the music, held a ministerial council, and had a notice prepared in his presence, to be signed by the prefect of police, which was pinned up at all street corners, saying: 'All seditious cries and cries of 'Long live the King' are forbidden, and anyone who starts them will be punished as a disturber of the public peace.'

A few days later it was learned that in the Palermo theatre and in the streets outside another demonstration had taken place, involving a rather larger number of people, to which it was decided to respond on the evening of December 14. . . . A large crowd turned up and shouted:

'Long live Palermo and Sicily.' . . . [Arrests were made.] In the royal palace the King did nothing but discuss police matters. . . . He frequently cursed Pius IX who had disturbed the hornet's nest, and expressed contempt for the weakness of Leopold [of Tuscany] and Charles Albert; mounting his high horse, he would say: 'I'll go and be a Colonel in Russia or Austria rather than yield and show weakness.' And he gave orders that students should be sent away from Naples, because they were full of new ideas, liable to get excited and quick on the draw. Immediately many poor young men were chased out at top speed. But everyone's irritation, curses and complaints were so great that the order was revoked. Could a government last long which knew neither how to be consistently bad nor genuinely good? . . .

[Settembrini was advised to leave the country, which he did on a British ship. After a few weeks in Malta, he returned to Naples on February 7, 1848.]

As the boat entered the harbour and prepared to anchor, I saw several ships with tricolour flags, in one of which was my brother Peppino, who shouted to me across the water: 'Constitution, amnesty. Bozzelli Minister of the Interior, Carlo Poerio[1] Director of the Police: everything is changed, disembark, disembark.' I embraced him and asked him: 'How has all this come about?' 'There was a great demonstration on January 27, and on the 29th was published the royal decree promising a constitution, and giving a full amnesty.' 'Was so much extracted by shouting?' 'In Naples there has been shouting, but in Palermo a terrible revolution which has defeated the troops, and a revolution in the Cilento.' 'And Ferdinand, who would rather be a colonel in Russia than yield, has yielded?' 'Yes, and as he signed the constitutional decree do you know what he said? "Don Pio Nono and Carlo Alberto wanted to trip me up with a stick, so I'll try this girder on them. Now let's all enjoy ourselves as best we can. . . ." '

When the King had the grievous news from Sicily, and felt the excitement in Naples growing daily, he asked the advice of those around him. Some said he should use cannon. Some said he should erect a gallows at the head of every street. Others said the use of force would irritate the people, and he must concede something to them; or that he must win over the liberals, and attach them to him with money, honours and even offices. All were agreed that the cause of all the trouble was the abuses of the police; they spoke of the dangerous power of Del Carretto, of his leaning towards the liberals, that he was reverting to the Carbonarism he had supported in 1820, that the Ministry of Police ought to be abolished. . . . On the night of January 26 Del Carretto was called to the royal palace as though to a council; he was brought into the presence of the Minister of War and General Carlo Filangieri, and they told him that by command of the King he must immediately . . . leave the Kingdom. . . .

Soon people were awaiting the constitution with impatience. Bozzelli

[1] Poerio was a noted conspirator who had only lately been in prison.

was compiling it by command of the King. Everyone imagined it as he wanted it himself, and some hastily wrote and printed proposals for a constitution, and hawked them about, and gave them to you to read, and asked: 'Will it do?' Old men said there was no need for a new constitution. That of 1820 would suffice, with a few slight modifications, thus affirming that the rights of the nation had never lapsed. This was the idea of the Sicilians, who were only interested in having the Constitution of 1812, brought up-to-date, but by Parliament and not by the King. On February 10 the King accepted the Constitution, on the 11th it was published. . . . The Constitution was [virtually] a copy, or rather a translation, of the French Charter of 1830. Bozzelli thought he had written the laws of Solon, which would immortalize him and make the people very happy. The multitude, without going into the matter further, started rejoicing as soon as it heard that the new law constituting the government had been published. They went to the front of the royal palace, and, although it was pouring with rain, they demanded to see the King and salute him. He appeared on the grand balcony. . . . The lower orders and the young, not knowing what they ought to say, and wanting to shout and perhaps mock, repeated 'Vivooo', a meaningless sound, because to them the change was meaningless. But words cannot indicate the emotions we felt at hearing many humble people shouting: 'Viva Italia! We are Italians!' That word 'Italy', which had at first been uttered by a few and in secret, which had been heard by only a handful, and which had been the last sacred word uttered by so many honourable men as they died—to hear it now uttered and shouted by the people made me feel a tingling run down my spine and through my body, and constrained me to tears. . . .

The gravest preoccupation for all was Sicily, which rejected the Neapolitan Constitution of February 10, and replied that it still wanted its own Constitution of 1812 . . . desiring to be an entirely separate and independent Kingdom, with a Viceroy who should be either a royal prince or a Sicilian citizen and should have the fullest powers; that the ministers should be nominated by the King but operate in Palermo, that there should be no more Neapolitan troops in Sicily, and that for dealing with affairs common to the two Kingdoms there should be established a mixed commission chosen from among the members of both Parliaments. These conditions seemed harsh not only to the King, but to a good many Neapolitans and Italians, who said and put in print that Sicily, in separating herself from Naples, would separate herself from Italy; that this 'Sicilianism' was unworthy, an ancient rancour between Palermo and Naples, the metropolis of the whole Kingdom; that brother nations ought to unite under the similar laws and institutions which produce similar customs and sentiments; that two constitutions would separate the two peoples more than the sea and for ever; that the Constitution of February 10 had been granted not on account of the shouts of Naples but of the blood of Palermo, and that they should accept it as their conquest. The Sicilians replied that they were not separating themselves from Italy, that their independence did no harm to Italy, which ought to unite as a federation and not into one Kingdom; that they had never lost their constitution since people never lose their rights, and now they had won it back with blood and not with shouts; that if Naples was a sister rather than a master, there would be no more rancour, no more occasion for hatred; that they knew the Bourbon and wanted none of the good that came from him; that they never wanted to see again in Sicily those dear brother Neapolitans who had bombarded their cities. . . .

The Ministry, which had not been able to find a way of settling the great question of Sicily, did not fall, but was transformed. . . . The revamped Ministry could not stop the excitement from daily growing. They broke up the great machine of the old government, but with little wisdom. They got rid of the bad, but they failed to find the good to put in their places. The rogues remained. The often inept substitutes did not know what to do. Everybody chattered, in the streets they complained of everything. They had won a constitution by shouting, so everyone thought he could get a job by shouting. In the clubs there was much talking about every subject under the sun, and those who talked fastest and aired the most fantastic plans were the most applauded. The Press, unrestricted, published scandal, calumny, truth, infamy, snapped at everyone. The masses said: 'And if there is no work, and we are starving, what liberty is that? Previously the King was one man, and ate for one; now they are a thousand, and they eat for a thousand. We also must look to our own situation.' In the provinces the peasants invaded and divided between them the lands belonging to the Crown, or to landlords who had earlier taken them over and were hated because they had got rich through usury and extortion. . . . And in the city of Naples the mob, not having lands to divide up, contemplated attacking and sacking houses as had been done in 1799. Into this confusion, like oil to a flame, came the accounts in the journals of the revolution and the republic in France, the movements which had now started in northern Italy, the constitution granted by Pius IX on March 13 because he couldn't do anything else, the expulsion of the Jesuits from Genoa. Henceforward people became crazy, the Constitution contented no one any more, and men said it was necessary to broaden it in order not to go so far as have a republic. . . .

In those March days there was revolution in Vienna, and Metternich fled. Milan rose, fought gloriously for five days and chased out the Austrians. The other Lombard cities rose, Venice rose to the call of Daniele Manin and drove out the foreigner, Modena and Parma rose. Charles Albert King of Piedmont hoisted the Italian flag and took an army into Lombardy. Revolution in Hungary, Bohemia, Bavaria, Saxony, Wurtemberg, Berlin, Poland, all over Germany. Europe opened up and burned like an immense volcano. Even today after so many years, when I recall so many miracles which began in Palermo on January 12, I feel my heart beating more strongly, and I say as I said then: 'It's no mere chance which moves at the same moment so many peoples of

Europe from Sicily to Jutland. This is the result of a long and secret process working in the consciousness of these peoples who have suffered the same evils. Will all this come to nothing? It is not possible. . . .'

A great crowd of people gathered in front of the royal palace and demanded that soldiers be sent into Lombardy. . . . Cristina Trivulzio, Princess of Belgioioso, a Milanese, who was then in Naples, offered herself as a guide to a group of zealous young men and left with them on March 29. Even from Sicily, implacable Sicily, came generous men who, forgetting all their grievances, made common cause with the Neapolitans . . . and went off with them to Lombardy. . . .

War against Austria was holy and necessary. But to want Ferdinand II to make that war was madness. To believe that he could be forced to make it was stupidity. . . . Either we had to remain Neapolitans, and not think of Italy, and be content with the Constitution of February 10 without going any further. Or, if we wanted to fight Austria, we had to broaden the Constitution and chase out Ferdinand, or at least take from him all the power he had over the army and leave him only the name of King. . . .

At the end of March, the whole Ministry, being unable to ride the tempest, resigned without having done any permanent good: not bad men, from many points of view deserving men, but incapable of governing in these storms. . . .

[The next Ministry, of Pepe, more radical, fell after the events of May 15, when the King reasserted his control against Parliament, Ministers and extremists with the aid of a popular reaction.]

13

Austrian Reaction and the Piedmontese Constitution

(TWO despatches from Abercromby, British Minister at Turin, to Palmerston, Foreign Secretary. From ed. F. Curato, *Le Relazioni diplomatiche fra la Gran Bretagna e il Regno di Sardegna*, III Serie: 1848–60, Vol. II, Rome, 1961, pp. 181–2, 210–13.)

A. *April 4, 1849*

... The hatred of the Austrians to the late King was so great, that they will be easy with his Son, for two reasons: first in the hope of firmly attaching him to them and to their policy, secondly from the desire of shewing their distrust and antipathy to the Father. For these reasons General Hess made no opposition to two out of the three points brought under rediscussion; and as regarded the reduction of the Sardinian army he admitted that it would, even in their sense, be impolitic to deprive the young King of the necessary means for preserving order in his own States, and the correctness of this opinion has unfortunately been speedily proved by the events of Genoa.

On the question of the amnesty for the Lombard emigrants, I found General Hess most positive and I am sorry to say illiberal. In his opinion but one method of governing Lombardy exists, and that is by the sword, and by ruling with a rod of iron. No argument appeared to produce any effect upon him, and it was with pain that I heard him assert, that exile from their Country was no punishment to a people. The General's policy evidently is, and I fear that his opinion has great weight, both with the Marshal and at Vienna, to attempt to crush completely the upper class of Lombards, to reject all measures of a conciliatory character, and to keep internal peace and tranquillity by inspiring terror. He may succeed in his plan so long as 80,000 Austrians continue unmolested to overrun Lombardy, but the day that France quarrels with Austria, or that the latter happens to be severely pressed upon from any other quarter, that moment Austria's tenure of Lombardy becomes again uncertain. For the present the issue of the late campaign has reestablished Austrian dominion in Lombardy, and over the greatest remaining part of Italy: but they have gained nothing upon the affections of the people, nor is the policy which they seem disposed to follow likely to lead to such a result.

The late campaign shews how correctly the Marshal was informed of all that was passing in this Country; or at least, how correctly he estimated the importance of the men he had to deal with; for nothing but the conviction of his success could otherwise have authorized the risk he was exposing himself to, by his invasion of Piedmont, and his movement upon Novara. He argued that one decided effort would prove sufficient to overthrow the King and his army, and to accomplish this he scraped together every man he could find, even down to the Custom House Officers, leaving only a garrison of 500 regular troops in Milan, and concentrating them under Pavia, he put his whole force across the Tessin in seven hours and opened his Campaign of three days.

No Austrians had actually moved upon Tuscany or the States of the Church when I was at Milan, but General Hess did not conceal his impatience to see some understanding come to by the Powers of Europe, for the final settlement of the affairs of those Countries. He said that if the accounts which they had of late received from Tuscany were deplorable, it was at least some consolation to know that matters were looking much better at Gaeta, where as he was assured, the Pope had come to the determination to be for the future entirely guided by the advice of Cardinals Antonelli, and *Lambruschini*. It would be superfluous in me to add another word upon this subject, after citing the General's opinion. . . .

The affair of Genoa is a great misfortune, and General de Asarta has been very culpable in giving up first two forts, and secondly in allowing himself to be driven out of the town. Genoa must now be recaptured, and troops are now marching upon it to reinforce La Marmora's Division.

The town and forts are all provisioned for several months to come as I am told; but if the acquaduct is cut, the town must surrender at discretion at the end of a few days, without having to fire a shot. The Decree of the state of siege of Genoa will be published today.

The Marquis Vincenzo Ricci came yesterday to me and to Bois le Comte for the purpose of inducing us to send a Secretary to Genoa to treat with the rebels, for fear of their pillaging the town: we however positively refused, and he was doomed to hear from us both, that the present disorders of Genoa were of his own creating, and that he was, as well as the rest of his colleagues, responsible for all the outrages that may be committed.

The rest of this Country is quiet; the Government are taking strong measures to reorganize the military, and reduce them to order, and if we can disband the Lombards without disorder, on the Emperor's amnesty being proclaimed, the interior of the King's States will very speedily regain its usual state of tranquillity. I should imagine it would be the wisest course for the Sardinian Government not to have the new elections until the peace shall have been concluded; and I shall consequently speak in that sense.

Money comes in readily enough, and the voluntary loan is filling up.

April 16, 1849

General De Launay sent for Monsieur Bois le Comte and myself this evening, to communicate to us the project of the treaty of peace proposed by Austria to Sardinia, and you will receive copy of it in my official letter of tomorrow. The declarations made to the Sardinian Plenipotentiaries at Milan by Monsieur de Bruck with respect to the amount of the war indemnity to be paid by Sardinia were of such a peremptory and unyielding nature, that they declared they could not undertake to come to any arrangement upon the subject, and that the question must be referred to the Government at Turin, and it was agreed that an answer should be given early on next Thursday morning. In the meanwhile Monsieur de Buoncompagni has returned to Turin to consult with the Government and to receive their instructions. A simple perusal of the Austrian project will suffice to let you know that only one answer can be given by Sardinia, *viz*: that to acquiesce in such a treaty is an utter impossibility. Such being the case, General De Launay called Monsieur Bois le Comte and myself together, and stated that it was the intention of the Sardinian Cabinet to declare the project proposed to be inadmissible, and that unless the pretentions of Austria were so materially reduced as to admit of being taken into consideration, Sardinia would be forced to seek the good offices, and support of her Allies. He said that he proposed if driven to that course, to send a special mission to Paris and to London for the purpose of stating to the Governments of England and France the situation in which Sardinia was placed, and the humiliating conditions which Austria was endeavouring to impose upon her, and of seeking their aid and assistance in this critical emergency; and he was anxious at the present moment to take our opinion as to whether he should despatch the special Mission at once, or wait to learn the effect which the communication of his intention may produce upon the Austrian Plenipotentiary. My French colleague and myself perfectly agreed in the expediency of not giving even the shadow of a pretext of complaint to Austria, and we both recommended that the mission should not be sent until after notice had been given to the Austrians. General De Launay then asked us to communicate to our Governments the state of affairs, and to warn them of the request which in all probability will be made to them; to this we consented, on his writing to us in that sense, which he has promised to do.

I do not attempt to point out any particular articles of this project for your observation; for there is not one in the whole treaty that is not objectionable, or which is not conceived for the purpose of humiliating this Country, and of reducing it to a state of vassalage to Austria. The articles respecting the limits; the naturalization of mixed subjects; the territory of Mentone and Roccabruna; the provisions for the surrender of all Venetian State property that may be carried off by Venetians; the demands in favour of Modena and Parma in addition to the 200 Millions for Austria, all speak for themselves; and the omission of all reference to an amnesty for the Lombards, even those included in the armistice of Novara, is equally significative. You will I feel convinced admit that no Government could meet a Sardinian Parliament and present such a treaty for its ratification. If therefore no modification of it can be obtained either by Sardinia alone, or by the assistance of her Allies, she has as it appears to me but one course left open for her, to declare that she will not accept such terms, to act solely on the defensive under the protection of the Armistice, and leaving to Austria the responsibility, if the provisional condition of the armistice is inconvenient to her, of recommencing hostilities with all the risks of entailing a war with France, which under such circumstances the latter will be forced to declare. I did not conceal from General De Launay that such was my opinion, and I strongly urged him and Monsieur Pinelli, who was present at the interview, not to do anything that should again place this Country in the false and prejudicial position from which it has just escaped.

The conversation then turned upon the question of the renewed threat of the Austrians to occupy Alexandria. After the plain and distinct assurances given by the Marshal and General Hess to General Dabormida and Count Revel, and subsequently to Monsieur de Bois le Comte and myself, as to their consenting not to require the execution of the Article concerning Alexandria, although they could not alter the Armistice itself, it would be a decided breach of good faith, which nothing could justify, if for the purpose of forcing this Country to accept ignominious terms, they were seriously to demand the fulfilment of this engagement. As however the threat has been renewed, General De Launay asked us what course we should advise the Government to take. I stated that it seemed to me that the honour and good faith of this Country were involved in the preservation of the sacredness of the Sovereign's signature and word of honour; that to refuse the execution of this engagement would probably entail a rupture of the armistice, and that the question of how far the Country was in a condition to renew the war, must be considered, because the results of a war might lead to a state of things even worse than the present; and Monsieur Bois le Comte and myself agreed in suggesting that if the Austrian Plenipotentiary should again revert to this question, that care should be taken to avoid giving any positive refusal to admit the joint occupation of Alexandria, but to say that the decision of this question should be referred as well as others to the Allies whose support had been requested. In short these people must manage if possible to ward off the occupation by raising discussion upon it, without giving Austria the benefit of a direct refusal to execute an engagement made.

The extreme illiberality of the Austrian project, and the attempt made to impose Austrian Dominion in its most odious form upon this Country, makes the course of the Government easy and clear, and they can appeal with confidence to the terms offered to them for a complete justification for the refusal to accept them. From your instructions to Lord Ponsonby of the 4th instant I see that you foresaw the course which Austria was likely to pursue and you will therefore not be surprised to learn from hence that your previsions have proved true. I therefore do not anticipate that you will decline to give all the assistance in your power to sustain a young Sovereign, whom it is attempted to oppress; but it is not England in this instance that can lend the most efficient help. France is the Power that must decide the fate of this Country; if she will act with firmness and energy in conjunction with us, Austria will not venture to kindle an European War, with Hungary unconquered, and the Russians in Transylvania; but if she is timid, Austria will bluster in proportion, and the consequences may be fatal to Piedmont and to Italy.

There is no disposition on the part of the Sardinian Government to avoid coming to a final arrangement with Austria; but at the same time they cannot agree to accept conditions to which they feel it would be impossible for the Country to submit without abandoning its honour and independence.

You will find ample proof in the Austrian Project of the intention to exercise an undue influence in the internal affairs of Sardinia, and so to cripple the Sovereign and his Government as to render them for the future powerless. By this project the King is called upon to abrogate Laws passed by the Parliament by simple Royal Decree, and were he to comply with the demands of Austria he would at the very commencement of his Reign have violated the Constitution he had just sworn to maintain. In short the terms now offered by Austria can only be described as an ingenerous attempt to crush a young Sovereign when in a moment of distress, and I sincerely hope that England and France by acting firmly and expeditiously together will prove that they have both the power and the will to resist oppression, while they at the same time take the surest means of avoiding the dangers of another appeal to arms. . . .

Plombieres

CAVOUR, from Baden-Baden, to Victor Emanuel, July 24, 1858. (Mack Smith, *The Making of Italy*, pp. 238–47.)

THE ciphered letter which I sent Your Majesty from Plombières could give only a very incomplete idea of the long conversations I had with the Emperor. I believe you will be impatient to receive an exact and detailed narration. That is what I hasten to do having just left France, and I send it in a letter via M. Tosi, attaché at our legation in Berne.

As soon as I entered the Emperor's study, he raised the question which was the purpose of my journey. He began by saying that he had decided to support Piedmont with all his power in a war against Austria, provided that the war was undertaken for a non-revolutionary end which could be justified in the eyes of diplomatic circles—and still more in the eyes of French and European public opinion.

Since the search for a plausible excuse presented our main problem before we could agree, I felt obliged to treat that question before any others. First I suggested that we could use the grievances occasioned by Austria's bad faith in not carrying out her commercial treaty. To this the Emperor answered that a petty commercial question could not be made the occasion for a great war designed to change the map of Europe. Then I proposed to revive the objections we had made at the Congress of Paris against the illegitimate extension of Austrian power in Italy: for instance, the treaty of 1847 between Austria and the Dukes of Parma and Modena; the prolonged Austrian occupation of the Romagna and the Legations; the new fortifications at Piacenza.

The Emperor did not like these pretexts. He observed that the grievances we put forward in 1856 had not been sufficient to make France and England intervene in our favour, and they would still not appear to justify an appeal to arms. 'Besides,' he added, 'inasmuch as French troops are in Rome, I can hardly demand that Austria withdraw hers from Ancona and Bologna.' This was a reasonable objection, and I therefore had to give up my second proposition; this was a pity, for it had a frankness and boldness which went perfectly with the noble and generous character of Your Majesty and the people you govern.

My position now became embarrassing because I had no other precise proposal to make. The Emperor came to my aid, and together we set ourselves to discussing each state in Italy, seeking grounds for war. It was very hard to find any. After we had gone over the whole peninsula without success, we arrived at Massa and Carrara, and there we discovered what we had been so ardently seeking. After I had given the Emperor a description of that unhappy country, of which he already had a clear enough idea anyway, we agreed on instigating the inhabitants to petition Your Majesty, asking protection and even demanding the annexation of the Duchies to Piedmont. This Your Majesty would decline, but you would take note of the Duke of Modena's oppressive policy and would address him a haughty and menacing note. The Duke, confident of Austrian support, would reply impertinently. Thereupon Your Majesty would occupy Massa, and the war could begin.

As it would be the Duke of Modena who would look responsible, the Emperor believes the war would be popular not only in France, but in England and the rest of Europe, because the Duke is considered, rightly or wrongly, the scapegoat of despotism. Besides, since he has not recognized any sovereign who has ruled in France since 1830, the Emperor need have less regard toward him than any other ruler.

Once we had settled this first question, the Emperor said: 'Before going further we must consider two grave difficulties in Italy: the Pope and the King of Naples. I must treat both of them with some circumspection: the first, so as not to stir up French Catholics against me, the second so as to keep the sympathies of Russia, who makes it a point of honour to protect King Ferdinand.'

I answered that, as for the Pope, it would be easy to keep him in possession of Rome by means of the French garrison there, while letting the provinces of the Romagna revolt. Since the Pope had been unwilling to follow advice over the Romagna, he could not complain if these provinces took the first occasion to free themselves from a detestable form of government which the Pope had stubbornly refused to reform. As for the King of Naples, there was no need to worry about him unless he took up the cause of Austria; but his subjects would be free to get rid of his paternal rule if the occasion offered.

This reply satisfied the Emperor, and we went on to the main question: what would be the objective of the war?

The Emperor readily agreed that it was necessary to drive the Austrians out of Italy once and for all, and to leave them without an inch of territory south of the Alps or west of the Isonzo. But how was Italy to be organized after that? After a long discussion, which I spare Your Majesty, we agreed more or less to the following principles, recognizing that they were subject to modification as the course of the war might determine. The valley of the Po, the Romagna, and the Legations would form a kingdom of Upper Italy under the House of Savoy. Rome and its immediate surroundings would be left to the Pope. The rest of the Papal States, together with Tuscany, would form a kingdom of central Italy. The Neapolitan frontier would be left unchanged. These four Italian states would form a confederation on the pattern of the German Bund, the presidency of which would be given to the Pope to console him for losing the best part of his States.

This arrangement seems to me fully acceptable. Your Majesty would be legal sovereign of the richest and most powerful half of Italy, and hence would in practice dominate the whole peninsula.

The question of what rulers would be bestowed on Florence and Naples was left open, assuming that the present incumbents, Your Majesty's uncle and cousin, would be wise enough to retire to Austria. Nevertheless the Emperor did not disguise the fact that he would like to see Murat return to the throne of his father; and, for my part, I suggested that the Duchess of Parma, at least for the time being, might take Florence. This last idea pleased the Emperor immensely. He appeared very anxious not to be accused of persecuting the Duchess of Parma just because she is a Bourbon princess.

After we had settled the fate of Italy, the Emperor asked me what France would get, and whether Your Majesty would cede Savoy and the County of Nice. I answered that Your Majesty believed in the principle of nationalities and realized accordingly that Savoy ought to be reunited with France; and that consequently you were ready to make this sacrifice, even though it would be extremely painful to renounce the country which had been the cradle of your family and whose people had given your ancestors so many proofs of affection and devotion. The question of Nice was different, because the people of Nice, by origin, language, and customs, were closer to Piedmont than France, and consequently their incorporation into the Empire would be contrary to that very principle for which we were taking up arms. The Emperor stroked his moustache several times, and merely remarked that these were for him quite secondary questions which we could discuss later.

Then we proceeded to examine how the war could be won, and the Emperor observed that we would have to isolate Austria so that she would be our sole opponent. That was why he deemed it so important that the grounds for war be such as would not alarm the other continental powers. Better still if they were also popular in England. He seemed convinced that what we had decided would fulfil this double purpose. The Emperor counts positively on England's neutrality; he advised me to make every effort to influence opinion in that country to compel the government (which is a slave to public opinion) not to side with Austria. He counts, too, on the antipathy of the Prince of Prussia toward the Austrians to keep Prussia from deciding against us. As for Russia, Alexander has repeatedly promised not to oppose Napoleon's Italian projects. Unless the Emperor is deluding himself, which I am not inclined to believe after all he told me, it would simply be a matter of a war between France and ourselves on one side and Austria on the other.

The Emperor nevertheless believes that, even reduced to these proportions, there remain formidable difficulties. There is no denying that Austria is very strong. The wars of the first Empire were proof of that. Napoleon Bonaparte had to fight her for fifteen years in Italy and Germany; he had to destroy many of her armies, take away provinces and subject her to crushing indemnities. But always he found her back on the battlefield ready to take up the fight. And one is bound to recognize that, in the last of the wars of the Empire, at the terrible battle of Leipzig, it was the Austrian battalions which contributed most to the defeat of the French army. It will therefore take more than two or three victorious battles in the valleys of the Po or Tagliamento before Austria will evacuate Italy. We will have to penetrate to the heart of the Empire and threaten Vienna itself before Austria will make peace on our terms.

Success will thus require very considerable forces. The Emperor's estimate is at least 300,000 men, and I think he is right. With 100,000 men we could surround the fortified places on the Mincio and Adige and close the Tyrolean passes; 200,000 more will be needed to march on Vienna by way of Carinthia and Styria. France would provide 200,000 men, Piedmont and the other Italian provinces 100,000. The Italian contingent may seem little, but you must remember that 100,000 effective front-line soldiers will mean 150,000 under arms.

The Emperor seemed to me to have well-considered ideas on how to make war, and on the role of each country. He recognized that France must have its chief base at La Spezia and must concentrate on the right bank of the Po, until we command the whole of the river and can force the Austrians into their fortresses. There would be two grand armies, one commanded by Your Majesty, the other by the Emperor.

Once agreed on military matters, we equally agreed on the financial question, and I must inform Your Majesty that this is what chiefly preoccupies the Emperor. Nevertheless he is ready to provide us with whatever munitions we need, and to help us negotiate a loan in Paris. As for contributions from other Italian provinces in money and material, the Emperor believes we should insist on something, but use great caution. All these questions which I here relate to you as briefly as possible were discussed with the Emperor from eleven o'clock in the morning to three o'clock in the afternoon. At three the Emperor dismissed me but gave me another appointment at four o'clock to take a drive with him.

At the agreed hour we got into an elegant phaeton drawn by American horses. The Emperor personally took the reins, and we were followed by a single servant. For three hours he took me through the valleys and forests which make the Vosges one of the most picturesque parts of France.

Hardly had we left the streets of Plombières when the Emperor broached the subject of the marriage of Prince Napoleon and asked what Your Majesty might think of it. I answered that you had been placed in a most embarrassing position when I communicated to Your Majesty the overtures made me by Bixio, because of doubts regarding the importance that he, the Emperor, attached to this matter. I reminded him of a conversation between Your Majesty and him in Paris in 1855 on the subject of Prince Napoleon and his project of marriage to the Duchess of Genoa, so that the whole issue was somewhat perplexing. I added that this uncertainty had increased as a consequence of Your Majesty's interview with Dr Conneau, who, when pressed by Your Majesty and myself, had declared not only that he had no instructions, but did not even know what the Emperor thought. I further added that, while wanting to do everything possible, you had a considerable repugnance to giving your daughter in marriage, because she was young and you could not impose an unwelcome choice upon her. If the Emperor strongly desired it, I added, you would not have irremovable objections to the marriage, but still wished to leave your daughter entirely free to choose.

The Emperor answered that he was very eager for the marriage of his cousin with Princess Clotilde, since an alliance with the House of Savoy was what he wanted more than anything else. If he had not instructed Conneau to discuss it, that was because he wanted first to know if such a proposal would be agreeable. As for the conversation with Your Majesty which I had cited, the Emperor first seemed not to remember it, and then after a while he said to me: 'I remember quite clearly having said to the King that my cousin had been wrong to ask the hand of the Duchess of Genoa; it seemed wrong that he should speak to her of marriage only a few months after her husband's death.'

The Emperor came back several times to the question of the marriage. Laughingly he said that he might sometimes have spoken ill of his cousin to you, for often he had been angry with him; but that at bottom he loved him tenderly since he possessed excellent qualities and for some time had been behaving in such a way as to earn the esteem and affection of France. 'Prince Napoleon,' he added, 'is much better than his reputation; he is a *frondeur*, he loves to be contrary, but he is witty as well as sensible, and he is warmhearted.' All this is true. That the Prince has intelligence you can judge for yourself, and I can confirm after many conversations I have had with him. That he has judgement is proved by his management of the Great Exhibition. Finally, that his heart is good is irrefutably proved by his constancy toward both friends and mistresses. A man without heart would not have left Paris amid the pleasures of carnival time to make a last visit to Rachel who was dying at Cannes, especially when they had separated four years earlier.

When answering the Emperor I tried not to offend him, yet I took pains to make no commitment. At the day's end when we separated, the Emperor said to me: 'I understand the King's repugnance at marrying his daughter so young; nor need the marriage be immediate; I am quite willing to wait a year or more if necessary. All I want is to have some kind of an answer. So please ask the King if he will consult his daughter, and let me know his intentions in a positive manner. If he consents to the marriage, let him fix the date. I ask no undertaking except our word, given and received.' With that we parted. Shaking my hand the Emperor dismissed me, saying: 'Have the same confidence in me that I have in you.'

Your Majesty will see that I have faithfully followed your instructions. As the Emperor did not make Princess Clotilde's marriage a *sine qua non* of the alliance, I did not assume the least engagement or obligation. But I beg you to let me express my frank opinion on a question upon which may depend the success of the most glorious enterprise which anyone has attempted for many years.

The Emperor did not make the marriage of Princess Clotilde with his cousin a *sine qua non* condition, but he showed clearly that it was of the greatest importance to him. If the marriage does not take place, if you reject the Emperor's proposal without good reason, what will happen? Will the alliance be broken? That is possible, but I do not believe it. The alliance will be made. But the Emperor will bring to it a quite different spirit from the one which he would have brought if, in exchange for the crown of Italy which he offers Your Majesty, you had granted him your daughter's hand for his nearest relative. If there is one quality which characterizes the Emperor, it is the permanence of his likes and his dislikes. He never forgets a service, just as he never forgives an injury. The rejection to which he has now laid himself open would be a blood insult, let there be no mistake about it. Refusal would have another disadvantage. We should then have an implacable enemy in the inner counsels of the Emperor. Prince Napoleon, even more Corsican than his cousin, would mortally hate us; the position he occupies, to say nothing of that to which he may aspire, as well as the affection and I would almost say the weakness the Emperor has for him, all this would give him many ways of satisfying his hatred.

Let us not deceive ourselves: in accepting the proposed alliance, Your Majesty and your kingdom bind themselves indissolubly to the Emperor and to France. If the war which follows is successful, the Napoleonic dynasty will be consolidated for one or two generations; if it fails, Your Majesty and your family run the same grave dangers as their powerful neighbour. But what is certain is that the success of the war and its glorious consequences for Your Majesty and your subjects depend in large part on the good will and friendship of the Emperor. If he is embittered against us, the most deplorable consequences could follow. I do not hesitate to declare my most profound conviction that to accept the alliance but refuse the marriage would be an immense political error which could bring grave misfortunes upon Your Majesty and our country.

But I know well that Your Majesty is a father as well as a King; and that it is as a father that you may hesitate to consent to a marriage which does not seem right and which is not of a kind to assure the happiness of your daughter.

Will Your Majesty let me consider this question not with the impassiveness of the diplomat but with the profound affection and absolute devotion in which I hold you?

I do not think people can say that the marriage of Princess Clotilde to Prince Napoleon is unsuitable. He is not a King, to be sure, but he is the first prince of the blood of the first Empire of the world. He is separated from the throne only by a two-year-old child. Your Majesty may well have to content yourself with a mere Prince for your daughter anyway, because there are not enough available Kings and hereditary princes in Europe. Prince Napoleon does not belong to an ancient sovereign family, but his father endowed him with the most glorious name of modern times; and through his mother, the Princess of Würtemberg, he is connected with the most illustrious princely houses of Europe. The nephew of the doyen of Kings, the cousin of the Emperor of Russia, is by no means a parvenu with whom it is shameful to be connected.

But the chief objections which can be made to this marriage lie perhaps in the personal character of the Prince and the reputation which he generally carries. On that subject I repeat with complete conviction what the Emperor said: he is better than his reputation. Thrown very young into the whirlpool of revolutions, the Prince was allowed to develop some very advanced opinions, and this fact, about which there is nothing extraordinary, has made him many enemies. The Prince has since then become quite moderate; but what does him great honour is that he remains faithful to the liberal principles of his youth while renouncing the application of them in any unreasonable or dangerous fashion, and that he has kept his old friends even when they were in disgrace. Sire, a man who when he attains the pinnacle of honour and fortune does not disavow those who were his companions in misfortune, and does not forswear the friendships he had among the defeated, such a man is not heartless. The Prince has braved the anger of his cousin to keep his old loves. He has never given in on this point, nor does he give in now. His generous words at the distribution of prizes at the Poitiers Exhibition are the proof of it. His conduct in the Crimea was regrettable. But if he could not stand the boredom and privations of a long siege, still he showed courage and coolness at the battle of Alma. Besides, he will make good on the battlefields of Italy the harm he did himself under the ramparts of Sebastopol.

The private life of the Prince may have sometimes been unsteady, but it has never given occasion for serious reproach. He was always a good son, and though he has angered his cousin more than once, still in serious matters he has always remained faithful and close.

Despite all this, I realize that Your Majesty may still hesitate and fear to compromise the future of your beloved daughter. But would she be more tranquil tied to an ancient princely family? History shows that princesses may be condemned to a sad life when they marry in accordance with propriety and ancient custom. To prove this I need not look far for an example, as I could instance what has happened recently in your own family.

Your Majesty's predecessor, Victor Emanuel I, had four daughters, models of grace and virtue. What became of their marriages? The first, the luckiest, married the Duke of Modena, a Prince who is universally detested. Surely you would not consent to a similar marriage for your daughter. The second married the Duke of Lucca. I need not remind you of the result of that marriage. The Duchess of Lucca was and is as unhappy as it is possible to be in this world. The third daughter, it is true, mounted the imperial throne, but that was for a husband who was impotent and imbecile, and who was obliged ignominiously to abdicate after a few years. Finally the fourth, the charming and perfect Princess Christine, married the King of Naples. Your Majesty certainly knows the gross treatment which she experienced, and the griefs which brought her to the tomb with the reputation of being a saint and martyr. In the reign of your father, another Princess of Savoy was married, your cousin Philiberte. Is she happier than the others, and would you wish the same fate for your daughter?

These examples show that in consenting to the marriage of your daughter to Prince Napoleon you would have a better chance of making her happy than if, like your cousin or your father, you married her to a prince of Lorraine or Bourbon.

But permit me a last reflection. If you do not agree to this marriage to Prince Napoleon, whom do you want her to marry? The Almanach de Gotha will show, as one might have expected, that there are no suitable princes. Religious differences prevent any alliance with most families who reign in countries with similar institutions to our own. Our struggle against Austria, our sympathy for France, makes impossible any marriage with families connected with the Houses of Lorraine or Bourbon. This reduces the choice to Portugal and a few more or less mediatized petty German principalities.

If Your Majesty will deign to meditate on these considerations, I dare flatter myself that you will recognize that as a father you can consent to this particular marriage, and that the supreme interest of the state, the future of your dynasty, of Piedmont, and of all Italy, advise its acceptance.

I beg your pardon for the liberty and the length of this report. In so important a question I could not be more reserved or more brief. The sentiments which inspire me and my motives will be enough to excuse my conduct.

Having had to write this endless epistle on a table at an inn without any time to copy it, nor even to reread it, I beg Your Majesty to be indulgent and forgive what disorder there may be in its ideas and the incoherence of its style. Despite these shortcomings, and because this letter contains a faithful and exact description of the communications which the Emperor made to me, I beg you to preserve it so that on return to Turin I can take notes from it which may serve in subsequent negotiations.

In the hope of being able, at the end of next week, to place at Your Majesty's feet the homage of my profound and respectful devotion, I have the honour to be Your Majesty's very humble and obedient servant and subject (*Il carteggio Cavour-Nigra*, Vol. I, pp. 103–10).

15

The Tuscan Revolution of 1859

(TRANSLATED from R. Ciampini, *Il '59 in Toscana*, Florence, 1959, pp. 40–2, 46, 54–6, 64–5, 161–2, 189–91, 276–7.)

A. *Count Carlo Boncompagni, Piedmontese representative in Florence, to Cavour, March 15, 1859.*

On my return to Tuscany I found people's minds more than ever occupied and excited by the idea of the national war which is thought imminent, while most of them, and especially the liveliest and most passionate part of the population, fail to appreciate the serious difficulties involved in a decision of this kind. In Leghorn I conferred at length with Signor Vincenzo Malenchini who has at his disposition a battalion of volunteers which he trained and holds in readiness for the arrival of the moment when this training can be useful to them. I think that H.M.'s Consul at Leghorn has already informed Your Excellency of the departure of about twelve young inhabitants of that town, intending to enrol in the army, who embarked from that port on the 12th of this month, and of the applause of the people who were present when they left. Malenchini, who at one time was in the camp of Montanelli, appeared most reasonable, and very willing to follow the lead of the Piedmontese Government. . . .

Here in Florence, too, many people are contemplating proceeding to the King's dominions in order to offer their services. Among them there are some young men from the most distinguished families, but they disdain enrolling themselves at the school in Ivrea. I have asked Captain Crespi to confer with them, so that they do not arrive in Piedmont with pretensions incompatible with regular military service. Otherwise I believe that the presence of these young men, and the names they bear, can help to show how favourable Tuscan opinion is to the Italian cause and to Piedmont which sustains it. These expressions of opinion favourable to us might be interrupted by the plan which some young men have made to stage a street demonstration hostile to the Prince and his Government. . . . I say to everyone that since the King and his Government have taken into their hands the care of the Italian cause, hostilities ought not to be provoked until they have given the order, and that the intentions of the Piedmontese government ought to be gathered from what I say myself, not from the speeches and letters of Tom, Dick and Harry.

It was also put to me that there was an idea of sending to Piedmont a considerable number of students of the University of Pisa. I did not accept, since this expedition would cause upheaval in families, would not be approved by the most responsible parties, and would not furnish a conclusive argument about the opinion of the country. . . .

On the part of those who, on account of age or for private reasons, are unable to take up arms, the most explicit sign that can be given of adhesion to the national cause is that of subscribing to provide the volunteers with the means to get themselves to Piedmont. The names of the subscribers are numerous and respectable. . . .

B. *Cavour to Boncompagni, March 20th.*

However little need there is for me to give you further information about the intentions of the King's Government, which are well known, nevertheless I exhort you and *charge you to use all your influence to prevent street demonstrations* and above all to avoid a collision with the troops of the Grand Duke. The former are almost always useless, and especially so now: in the great enterprise for which Italy is preparing, it is desirable that we shun the errors of 1848 and 1849, among which, and not least, ought to be numbered the disorderly shouting of multitudes. Once the push has been given, it is very difficult to hold back the most enthusiastic. Making a tumult becomes a habit, and those who are brought up to it come to think that with their slogans and their processions they have made a sufficient offering of courage, perseverance and sacrifice. . . .

C. *Boncompagni to Cavour, April 3, 1859.*

Here there are again appearing signs of a desire for demonstrations. . . . The Government on its side seems to be looking for ways of getting up a demonstration favourable to itself; there has been talk of a great military review in which the troops would be asked to proclaim *Long live the Grand Duke.* I do not believe that this plan will go forward, because with the national idea so widely diffused in the army it would probably be a fiasco. Some people speculate that there is an intention to evoke a favourable demonstration among the peasants, who made such at the time of the French Revolution and in 1849. . . .

In the last few days Count Giovanni Malvezzi and his brother-in-law Marquis Luigi Tanari have arrived here from Bologna, and they are still in this city. They have come to confer with me on the object of the demonstration Your Excellency desires in the Romagna, which would be the equivalent in that province of what has been done in Tuscany with the publication of the pamphlet *Tuscany and Austria*. . . . These gentlemen entirely agree with us on the timeliness of an event calling the attention of Europe to the Papal State, and this will be arranged as soon as it readily can be. . . .

From what they told me I had to acknowledge that the National Society of La Farina had been and perhaps could still be the cause of disagreements among the Liberals of Bologna. Malvezzi, Bevilacqua and a good many others of the principal citizens of that city who have always supported the liberal party, viewed it with suspicion on account of the opinions formerly expressed by La Farina, and with jealousy because they feared that it aimed to take over sole direction of the country. Tanari and Casarini with whom we conferred in Turin belong to a more advanced section, and therefore back the National Society . . . . I said to Count Malvezzi that at this moment no one's past life and opinions should be enquired into; that the Piedmontese Government was employing the National Society as a useful instrument of its policy; that the Piedmontese Government will never deviate from its principles, liberal and conservative at one and the same time; that it has great respect for those who in the various provinces have special authority because of the rank they hold and the services they have already rendered to the liberal and Italian cause. . . .

D. *Marquis de Ferrières, French representative in Tuscany, to Count Walewski, French Foreign Minister, May 18, 1859.*

Since the events of April 27th [the flight of the Grand Duke], a certain uneasiness weighs on people's minds. Florence is astounded, perhaps even more than on the first day, by this sudden disappearance of the royal family; and the bond of protection that has been improvised through the force of circumstances between Tuscany and Sardinia has produced a feeling of distrust and even humiliation. Men fear that they will cease to be Tuscan and become Sardinian; and people who seemed to desire annexation a month ago, out of opposition to the Grand Duke, now appear anxious to preserve autonomy. M. Boncompagni was saying to me on this point: 'I have never found my friends so Florentine as since I have been the King's Commissioner at Florence.'

E. *Ferrières to Walewski, July 26, 1859.*

The revolution of April 27th had been held within the limits of a certain moderation and I had secured that the provisional government did not declare the Grand Duke deposed or compromise its autonomy. M. Boncompagni had taken the same line; and the spirit of the people had not developed beyond the habitual calm and mildness of the Tuscans until the arrival of the 5th Corps of the Army of Italy [under Prince Napoleon]. Then followed great pressure from the Piedmontese Government on the Tuscan Government. The lawyer Salvagnoli entered the Ministry, and claimed that it was necessary to agitate the country vigorously on behalf of annexation and that this was the Emperor's wish. It was at this date that the revolution really began. All the troops were carried off, and the population was left, weak and feeble, at the mercy of the clubs, without a soldier to protect them. No blood was shed, there was no disorder evident, because there was no resistance. But the current of the unionist idea dragged the uncertain along with it, submerged the frightened and cut itself a huge bed, exerting a fascination on people's minds by its very success. I saw some strange recantations emerge from informed and important men. I send to Your Excellency the two letters attached, to inform you about this anodyne terrorism, carried out silently and at little expense, but as effectively as if it had burned and killed, operating on a mild people who have become unfamiliar with revolutionary proceedings over a period of three centuries. Baron Ricasoli has been the inflexible and unscrupulous agent of this regime of terror, and there is good reason to be surprised, when one knows the true state of things, that in his last report to M. Boncompagni he should praise the freedom and spontaneity of the municipalities' votes in favour of annexation—since nearly a hundred *gonfalonieri* have been deprived of office and replaced by people of his persuasion, and several municipal councils, including that of Siena . . . resigned the day after their vote in protest against the violence to which they had been subjected. . . .

When I have tried to sound out the position, and spoken of Archduke Ferdinand and the possibility that the Emperor might wish to see him recalled by the national assembly, the most moderate and reasonable men have assured me that nothing could now stop the vote to depose him. . . .

The assembly will be unionist, but especially anti-dynastic. People hope at least to avoid having an Archduke again, and, if autonomy is preserved, they aim at enlarging Tuscany from the Duchy of Modena and the Legations. . . .

F. *Marquis Spinola, acting for Boncompagni, to Count Dabormida, Piedmontese Foreign Minister, August 5, 1859.*

Yesterday I made an official visit to the French Minister . . . who advised restoration, since the instructions he had received ordered him to do so, and since he did not see what better choice Tuscany had. He stressed that, as regards annexation to Piedmont, the Emperor did not want to hear of it, England opposed it, and the King had taken it upon himself to refuse the offer. I thought it prudent not to enter into this thorny question, and I committed myself as little as possible, confining myself in reference to England to drawing his attention to the latest speech made by Lord Russell in the House of Commons. . . .

Montanelli pushes the candidature of Prince Napoleon. . . .

G. *Count de Mosbourg, French representative in Florence, to Count Thouvenel, French Foreign Minister, March 7, 1860.*

In four days time the vote will take place. The result is not in doubt. It will be favourable to annexation. It is even said that the opposition will not make a fight of it, and will show itself only in abstentions. . . . The

Government has resolved to proclaim the freedom of the Press. . . . But this measure, taken so near the date fixed for the trial, is virtually illusory. An opposition cannot possibly organize itself in a few days. . . . Public opinion has been moulded. There is no positive constraint; the Government has no material force at its disposal, and one cannot say that the means of influence it uses go so far as menace or intimidation. But the present situation is the product of the skilful and energetic exercise of authority over a period of ten months. . . .

16

Cavour and Garibaldi's Expedition

Cavour to Emanuele d'Azeglio, Sardinian Minister in London, July 12, 1860.

In Sicily, Garibaldi has let himself become intoxicated with his success. Instead of carrying annexation, or allowing it to be carried, he dreams of conquering Naples and delivering Italy. If moderating counsels came to him from England, for which he has great respect, that would be most advantageous. I know the Minister cannot put himself in direct contact with Garibaldi; but he could indoctrinate the Admiral, who seems to me to be a man of much tact and authority.

Annexation would get us out of an embarrassing situation, because it would bring Garibaldi back into a regular position. If annexation is delayed, I foresee the greatest difficulties.

As for Naples, . . . I do not yet know precisely what I shall say. If they would really consent to cede Sicily, and would help us to demolish Rome, I believe that we could come to an agreement, at least for a time. . . .

FROM *Cavour e l'Inghilterra*, Vol. II, Tome II (Bologna, 1933), pp. 93–4.

Cavour and Garibaldi's Expedition

Index